Value Your Children

Value Your Children

Becoming Better Parental Disciple-Makers

Kirby Worthington
and
Everett L. Worthington, Jr.

Strategic Christian Living

Baker Books

A Division of Baker Book House Co
Grand Rapids, Michigan 49516

Published by Baker Books
a division of Baker Book House Company
P.O. Box 6287, Grand Rapids, MI 49516-6287

Printed in the United States of America

Library of Congress Cataloging-in-Publication Data

Worthington, Kirby.
    Value your children : becoming better parental disciple-makers /
Kirby Worthington and Everett L. Worthington, Jr.
      p. cm.
    Includes bibliographical references.
    ISBN 0-8010-5401-X (paper)
    1. Family—Religious life. 2. Parenting—Religious aspects—Chris-tianity. 3. Child rearing—Religious aspects—Christianity. I. Wor-thington, Everett L., 1946–   II. Title.
BV4526.2.W67 1996
248.8′45—dc20

                                                        95-36902

To
Our parents, Clyde and Rena Canipe, and Everett and
Frances Worthington, who valued us and taught us of
Christ's love, and
Our beloved children, Christen, Jonathan, Becca, and
Katy Anna, who have made parenting a joy.

Contents

Acknowledgments

We are grateful to Karen Bowles and Jackie Bolt, and other dear family members and friends, who read and commented on our early drafts, who have shared their stories with us, prayed with us, and helped us grow.

We also thank our Lord for our pastor, Doug McMurry, who stressed that love is choosing to value and not to devalue. That central theme of this book, we learned from him.

1

Helping Your Child

Mary and Jim[1] needed help with their parenting. Their two boys, only a year apart, argued incessantly. They openly defied their parents. Sunday school teachers dreaded Sunday morning's ordeal of facing both boys in a small room—unarmed! Baby-sitters suddenly had something to do when Mary called—like counting dust nurdles in their rooms. School authorities wrote home weekly about at least one boy's misbehavior. The boys were out of control, wild, undisciplined.

Mary and Jim were emotional wrecks. Jim had been raised in a permissive home and had difficulty disciplining the boys until they became so disruptive that he lost his temper, lashing out sarcastically or yelling. Mary was raised strictly but was taught that the father should be the disciplinarian, so she said nothing until she too finally exploded. Both Jim and Mary felt angry with the boys, and the anger spilled over into their marriage.

Tensions escalated. Jim spent most of his time at work. Mary became withdrawn, and with even less supervision, the boys acted up even more. One day Jim came home and found Mary crying—as she had been for three hours. Mary had to be hospitalized.

1. Throughout the book, names and details have been changed to safeguard identities.

At the hospital they met Pastor Dan, a retired pastor doing chaplaincy, who ministered hope to Jim and Mary. Both renewed a long-shelved commitment to Jesus. When Mary was released from the hospital, she and Jim began to attend a church that Pastor Dan had recommended. The church was a healing balm. Jim and Mary were taken into a fellowship of love by new friends and a loving pastor. Jim and Mary searched the Scriptures, discussed child-rearing with their pastor and friends, and prayed. Jim accepted the God-given commands for him to train and discipline his children in love, and Mary learned that discipline was not just Jim's job, but was a team effort.

At first, the boys bucked at the changes. They had run the show for years and weren't about to give up control without a struggle. But Mary and Jim were faithful to their new vision of parenting, and as they worked at consistent parenting in faith and love, the children felt more secure and began to control their disruptive behavior (except for an occasional prank like putting pepper in Jim's coffee).

Jim and Mary cared. Jesus cared and placed them in the path of Pastor Dan, other Christians, and a new pastor— all of whom also cared. Care, which is love in action, works miracles.

You care about your child and want to help with his or her problems. Your willingness to tackle a book to help you parent more effectively attests to your love for your child.

You Care Enough to Be a Better Parent

Fear whispers to parents, "It's too hard to change." "I've always lost my temper. I can't control it." "I'm too tired." "What if I try and fail?" Don't listen to fear. Dare to change. We know you care enough, and we want to make it easier to solve whatever problems you have. Following are 13 steps that will help prepare you to walk that challenging road of change.

Step 1: Realize That You're Not Alone

Carly wiped tears from her cheek with the back of her hand. After having poured out her frustrations and failures at disciplining five-year-old Jossey, she sat slump-shouldered and listened intently as Kirby described how other good parents have struggled with similar problems.

"I felt so alone," she said. "It helps to know that others have had the same troubles." The beginning of healing was finding that others had walked in Carly's shoes. Others have shared your struggles, too.

Step 2: Admit Your Problems

We don't want others to know our imperfections because we think they might look down on us. The Bible says, "Confess your sins to each other and pray for each other so that you may be healed," (James 5:16 NIV). If you admit your sins, mistakes, and needs to the Lord, and to people you trust—counselor, pastor, friend, or relative—then you can begin to be helped.

Step 3: Examine Yourself before God

Pastor Larry Christenson (1970) calls this step of self-examination "empathetic repentance" (see Rom. 2:3–4; Matt. 7:1–5). When you see some behavior or attitude in your children (or in anyone else) that bothers you, ask God to show you where in your own life you may be guilty, even in a small way, of that same sin. When God shows you, ask for forgiveness and for his help to stop it, to cleanse you, and to set you free. Ask forgiveness also of those you've hurt with that sin.

One of our children went through a period of arguing with everything we said. At times, we argued back, lost our tempers, and worried. Eventually, we remembered "empathetic repentance." God showed us times that we had not respected our children, had wanted our own selfish way and had gotten it because we were bigger. We too had argued to win so that we would feel powerful. We told our children what God had shown us, asked God and our children to forgive us, and prayed for the Lord to show us each time we devalued a child to get control. Our confession freed us to value our children more and peace soon returned. While we were training our children, our heavenly Father was training us to be more like Jesus.

Step 4: Examine Your Motivation

Ask, "Do I really *want* to solve this problem?" A recently remarried friend told Kirby that her son was having trouble in school, had seen the school counselor, and was now seeing a psychiatrist for emotional problems. The friend complained of tremendous stress because her job gave her no time for herself, her child, or her new husband.

"Have you considered cutting your hours to part-time to reduce the stress?" Kirby asked, knowing that her friend's husband had a good job.

"No," she answered, "I like the extra money too much." She wanted relief, but not enough to change.

Before you can solve your problems, you must want to change. Even little changes require effort. Ask yourself, "Am I willing to change my habits to help my family?"

Step 5: Catch Problems Early

Most problems, if caught early, can be easily solved. Allowed to continue, problems grow unruly. Parents know that, but sometimes they don't act on their knowledge. It seems easier to let a problem go.

- "I'm too tired."
- "This is just a stage."
- "The problem will go away on its own."

- "It isn't so bad."
- "Other kids do it."

In the long run, it takes less energy to deal with a new problem than to let it slide until it becomes an ingrained habit.

Step 6: Set Realistic Goals

After you have decided to change, don't try to change everything at once. For example, if you decide to correct less and compliment more, you might set the goal, "I will tell Sally something good she has done or comment on one of her good qualities at least once every day. I'll write a note on the aspirin bottle to remind myself." Or you might want to spend more time with your child. A realistic goal might be, "I will read 15 minutes with Tim two times this week. I'll put it on the calendar." Don't set your initial goals so high that they discourage you.

Step 7: Be Patient; Change Takes Time and Hard Work

You may be fearing, "Even if I set goals, things might not get better. So why try?" We cannot promise that you will solve all of your child's problems. We can promise you that if, with God's help and your effort, you *try*, then you and your child will benefit. Try for an extended period, not just a couple of days. Long-practiced behaviors won't change overnight. You'll have setbacks. Admit them, ask forgiveness, and *try again*. Don't give up. God won't.

Step 8: Change What You Can

Try as hard as we may, we can't change anyone else's behavior. We can only change our own, and if we are fully honest, we must admit that we can't even change our own behavior without God's help. Nonetheless, parents often act as if they thought they could change their children. They can't. Parents can train, but only God can change people.

You can, however, work responsibly to change what you can. God empowers you to

- change your own parenting behavior to bring it more into conformity with God's will (ask God to help you see yourself honestly so you can change);
- learn all you can about how children develop;
- value your children and avoid devaluing them;
- love your children, in words and actions, and teach them how to show love to others;
- teach your child how to honor you;
- arrange your home-life to make it likely that your children will seek the Lord and act responsibly; and
- pray daily to a great God who has great power.

Remember your goal, of allowing God to change *you*, throughout the trials of dealing with your children's problems.

Another aspect of changing what you can is asking God to help you re-see behaviors in your child that irritate you. Some qualities that drive you up a wall now may actually be unpolished gifts from God.

Activity: Try to see each child with new eyes. Ask God to show you what each child contributes to the family. For example, in one family there may be a child who always keeps the family waiting. He or she may pay such attention to detail that getting dressed takes four days and every project takes an eternity. When you're tired and irritated, you might call that pickiness, vanity, or procrastination. But ask God for a new view. He made that child with that temperament. His good plan may have gotten warped and need curbing, but look at the underlying quality. What good can come from such a quality? Does such a child help a hurried family slow down and breathe, for example? Write your insights. Praise your child for the good side of qualities when you see them.

Step 9: Be Willing to Make Mistakes

All parents want to be perfect—never making mistakes and always disciplining effectively and teaching perfectly. Perfectionism paralyzes. Parents cannot know every correct decision. That's good. We can then rely on God rather than on ourselves or on a set of rules. God provides direction. Parenting is like sailing. We move back and forth across that godly direction, like a sailboat tacking, until we arrive where God wants us. But we can only arrive where God wants us if we courageously try new ways, make mistakes, and listen to God correct those mistakes.

Step 10: Small Changes Make Big Differences

If your child is having difficulties, your heart desires a solution. You probably visualize reading this book, attending a counseling session or two in which you receive sage advice, and applying THE SOLUTION, which will completely transform your child. After all, it happens in the movies, right?

Think of change differently. Imagine standing in Los Angeles looking toward Boston. You want to move East, but you decide that you want a warmer climate than Boston, so you change direction by one degree. By the time you arrive at the East coast, you'll be far south of Boston.

Life is a journey across time. Your objective is to help your child mature, and you will achieve more by reorienting your child by a single degree in his or her basic direction than by trying to carry your child into adulthood. When you try to control your child by power plays, that's like carrying him or her. You can't carry another human being very far without collapsing. Even if you could carry your child, he or she couldn't walk when you arrived. Let your child travel the road with you and God as guides, not as carriers. Rejoice in small changes, trusting God to enlarge them as your child travels.

Step 11: Do What Works

When I smash my finger in a door, it hurts continually. Every time I touch anything, I recoil. I arrange my life to avoid pain, and I think constantly about what I *can't* do with a hurt finger. Similarly, if your child has problems, it is easy to think constantly about the problems, to focus on the failures, to dwell on the disappointments.

To solve the problems, change your focus. What are you doing, or what have you done that has worked? Don't say, "Nothing." That's discouragement talking. Everyone—even the most discouraged parents with the most difficult children—are doing and have done many things effectively. Rediscover those things, then do them. Do things together that you used to love. Revive love between you and your children by making dates to cuddle and read, take walks in the park, roll in the leaves, visit the zoo, ride a bus, go skating or bike riding. Fun and laughter together set you on the path toward healing and open everyone to work together to restore joy.

Step 12: Get a Buddy

To stay motivated and encouraged, ask God to help you find a same-sex parent and reveal your plans to change. If your prayer partner has children of similar ages to your own, you can help each other. However, don't close out the possibility of an older or younger friend who is in a different stage of family life. You can find great treasures and wisdom in different ages. Ask your friend to pray with you regularly, by phone or in person, and to hold you accountable by asking how it's going (Eccles. 4:9–10). At today's fast pace, you may need to set time limits with your prayer partner and stick to them. Some parents pray over the phone with their prayer partners for 15 to 30 minutes before they wake their children. Some choose one evening each week. Regardless, be open, vulnerable, and consistent in prayer and support.

Step 13: Commit to Pray Daily for Each Child

Prayer is a parent's most powerful tool. Pray daily for each family member. If you are not in the habit of praying for your children, use daily reminders. Attach rubber bands to your toothbrush or let the act of plugging in your coffee pot remind you to plug into the Lord.

Tailor the time of day to your habits. Some pray (eyes open) as they drive to work. Some pray at night. We wake at 5:30 each morning to have time with the Lord before things get hectic, and we pray a blessing over each child as he or she leaves for school. We often lay our hands gently on our children's heads and pray for them, after they are asleep at night. (This was easier when they were younger and went to bed before we did. Now that three of the four are teenagers, we are often in bed before they are. I wonder if they now pray over us as we sleep.)

Some parents pray together, some pray with a prayer partner, some pray separately. Do what's best for you. Whatever method or time of prayer you choose, make prayer a daily priority. If we do nothing else in this book, we so desire to encourage you (and remind ourselves) to not turn to techniques by themselves, but to turn to the only perfect Father and ask his help, wisdom, and power to raise your children. Don't try to parent without him. As you pray, not only will lives be changed, but so will your relationship with the Lord.

Activity: Read again the 13 steps in preparing to change your parenting. Mark each step you've already taken. Are

there any you haven't yet risked? Pray that God will give
you the courage, knowledge, and wisdom to take those
steps and that he will help you grow into a more faithful disciple of Jesus Christ.

Get Down to Specifics

The above 13 steps bring you to the threshold of this
book. Like Dorothy in Oz, through little fault of her own,
standing before a doorway that leads into a new multicol-
ored world, you are poised on the brink of working systematically to change yourself, to alleviate your child's difficulties, and to help both your child and yourself grow into
more mature Christians.

Like Dorothy, you must travel the yellow brick road not to
visit the humbug of Oz, but the true emperor—the God of
heaven—face-to-face. Like Dorothy, you have been provided
worthy companions—perhaps a spouse, family members,
friends, and children—who will be fellow travelers. Like
Dorothy, you must face the nightmare of the Wicked Witch of
the West in the form of the problems that plague you and your
child, and you must battle those problems intentionally and not
simply hope that a house will fall on them. Like Dorothy, you'll
discover many things about yourself and your fellow travelers
on the journey. At the end of L. Frank Baum's story, Dorothy
had matured. That is your destination—maturity in the Lord.

2

The Cause of the Problem

I hate you!" "Get out of my sight—you make me sick."
"You'll never amount to anything." Similar words may echo
from your childhood and threaten to burst out when you
are tired or irritated. It's easy to recognize that these hurtful statements are not Christ's plan. But what is his plan?

Christ's pattern for how we should parent our children
is fundamental. Every form of discipline and any teaching
techniques that parents use must be governed by Christ's
plan, shown in Scripture. Problems arise in families because
either children or parents or both deviate from God's pattern for Christian living. This fundamental pattern is *faith
working through love.*

In Galatians 5:6, people are told, "For in Christ Jesus neither circumcision nor uncircumcision is of any avail, but
faith working through love" (RSV). In the NIV, this is trans-
lated, "For in Christ Jesus neither circumcision nor uncircumcision has any value. The only thing that counts is faith
expressing itself through love." If faith working through
love is "the only thing that counts," then it must be important to understand and do.

21

This principle, living by faith working through love, is fundamental guidance for Christian living given throughout Scripture. Parenting is an important part of Christian living. Let's look at each part of this command to exercise faith working through love. We will begin with "love" because defining love is essential to understanding faith and work.

Love

Definition of love. We define love as choosing (an act of the will) to value others and choosing not to devalue them. This definition of love is evident throughout the Bible.

Love in the Bible. Jesus' life testifies to this principle. Jesus loved us by giving his life for us. He valued people more than his own life. According to Christ, love is not merely a good feeling, though it involves feelings. For example, Jesus told people to love their enemies (Luke 6:27–35), which can't be done from feelings. Love is an act of the will. If parents love their children, parents must decide to treat them as valuable.

The Old Testament equates loving children with valuing them. Psalm 127:3 says, "Children are a gift from the Lord. They are a real blessing!" (TEV). God's gifts are of great worth.

In 1 Corinthians 13, all of the statements describing love boil down to one thing: love is valuing the needs of the loved one more than one's own needs. "Love is patient . . . kind. It does not envy. . . . It is not rude . . . not self-seeking . . . not easily angered, it keeps no record of wrongs" (NIV).

Activity: Stop and prayerfully read 1 Corinthians 13:4–8 in several different versions. Ask God to show you where you have not acted in valuing love toward your children. Ask his forgiveness and he will gladly forgive (1 John 1:9). Then invite the Lord to build his love into you.

When your child isn't lovable. When the New Testament writers say to love even the unlovely, God expects us to obey (Matt. 5:44–46; 19:19; 22:39; Luke 6:27–35; John 13:35; 15:17; Rom. 13:10; Eph. 4:2). Sometimes parents may feel that their children are acting unlovely, or even acting like enemies. Like the time Jeremy was angry. He let your prize parakeet out and the cat ate it. Or when Melissa screamed, "You're ugly and stupid. You never let me do what I want to." That doesn't let parents off the hook. Parents are told to value their children, even if they seem like unlovely enemies.

God can give parents the power to keep loving an unlovable child until the child is healed enough to respond in more loving ways. As the child is encouraged and valued, prayed for, and consistently trained with clear rules and fair rewards and punishments, the child will become increasingly easier to love.

Jesus said, "Love your enemies, do good to those who hate you, bless those who curse you, pray for those who abuse you. . . . And as you wish that men would do to you, do so to them. If you love those who love you what credit is that to you? . . . but love your enemies and do good . . . for he (God) is kind to the ungrateful and the selfish. Be merciful, even as your Father is merciful" (Luke 6:27, 28, 31, 32, 35 RSV). If Jesus expects people to show such kindness to their enemies, shouldn't parents treat their children as well as Christ tells them to treat an enemy?

> **Activity:** Write five things your child does that you value. The next time you see him or her doing each activity, praise the child.

Value-Given-and-Received Cycle

As long as people receive love, they can usually give love. If they are devalued, they often devalue in return. When baby Jerod cuddled and smiled during the day, his parents felt valued and could put up with night feedings and diaper changes. But when two-year-old Shelly threw frequent tantrums, her parents felt devalued and loving wasn't as easy. When a child or teen is warm and talks about his or her day, tells jokes and hugs the parents, parents feel valued and overlook occasional arguing; but if the teen sulks, snaps, or is moody and withdrawn, parents feel devalued and may develop a short fuse that explodes easily.

Harsh, devaluing words and cold shoulders from children drain parents of the energy to love. If you see how devaluing affects you, an adult, then you can see how devaluing words and actions and belittling punishment can rob children of energy they need to love.

Children get their early ideas of who they are, their self-worth, from their parents. If parental words and actions say, "You are very important—more valuable to me than a million jewels, my favorite TV show, or golf. I love being with you. God created you for a special purpose, and I can see much good in you," then children feel valued, see themselves as having worth, and will in turn value their parents.

If parents don't help their children find worth, children seek it from other sources, some of which may destroy them. Parents need to help their children find the real source of their worth in God. Children have great worth in God's eyes.

If parents have received God's love and forgiveness it is easier for them to give love and forgiveness to their children. If children receive love from their parents, it is easier for them to receive what Jesus offers them and for them to give love back to their parents. *Love received can be given.*

Love is choosing to value and not to devalue your children. You can decide to treat them daily as pearls of great value, just as Jesus sees you and them. Sometimes pearls are in hardened shells, hidden deeply, and covered with mud, but that doesn't change their value. Parents can choose, with God's help, not to let the shell or mud change their decision to treat their children as valuable.

Do you see the difficult but exciting challenge God puts before parents? God wants parents to draw close to him and receive his healing and love. Parents need to recognize where they have devalued or not valued their children, pray for their children daily, and discipline with valuing love and prayer to help their children become more like Christ.

> **Question:** Write a specific time that you put down or devalued your child. How could you have acted differently that would have treated your child as a pearl of great value?

Failure in Love

Check our motives. To show valuing love to our children, it is helpful to examine some hindrances. Sometimes what we *think* is showing love is perceived differently by our children. Sometimes what we think is effective discipline, is actually our own explosion because we were inconvenienced or our attempt to gain control because we are anxious.

Getting kicked about after a soccer match. Here is a recent example of a failure in love that we observed. After one soccer match, there was a misunderstanding about pick-up time and the coaches had to wait late for parents to arrive, delaying many other girls who needed to be dropped off at different locations. One coach berated the girls and humiliated them in front of their teammates, yelling at them about responsibility. The girls were truly sorry that they were holding everyone up, but the more the coach blew up at them, the less repentant and the more angry they became. Afterwards one girl said, "No one did wrong on purpose. It was a mistake, and no one deserves to be treated like that. That coach doesn't deserve an apology." Rather than anger and put downs, the coach might better have calmly said, "We have to get these other girls back to their parents. We want to get home to our families, too. But we cannot leave you here alone. I'm sure there is a reason your parents are late, but we have a problem. Can you help us think of a solution? Is there any adult you can call to come wait with you until your ride arrives?" That would have created an atmosphere of cooperation rather than of resistance and anger.

Let's apply this situation to the family. A child's repentance may only come if you, the adult, treat the child with understanding and valuing love. God made each person with an inner core to give and receive valuing love. When such love is not given, it hurts. When people are devalued, they often build a protective shell around that inner, vulnerable core, to try to stop the pain.

Protecting the inner core. Two strategies are often used to try to protect the inner core—those that *attack* others (such as the coach berating the girls) and those that *defend* the self (the girls became defensive, resistant, and noncooperative). Both strategies devalue others.

Attacks include put downs that devalue the other person—looks, sighs, cruel jokes, straight words of criticism, digs, zingers, and tirades of yelling about the other's failures. Public attacks are the most devastating. You can probably recognize when you've used some of these. Other devaluing habits (like looks, sighs, and jokes) are harder for parents to recognize in themselves. Ask your spouse or your children to help you recognize when you have devalued them in ways you may not realize. Be careful not to react defensively when they do what you've asked. Ask your children to gently remind you, "Mama, you said you wanted me to tell you when you put me down with a look. You just did." Reply, "Thank you for telling me. I want to stop. I love you and don't want to put you down. This will help me recognize when I do it. Please forgive me." Then make every effort to stop the hurtful behavior.

Attack power strategies usually come in a series. They start mild, then become more intense, if no one stops them. An example of a mild attack could be when one person arranges to do things his or her own way, but presents it in a way that others dare not question. The attacker often is unaware that he or she is making others feel attacked or controlled. The person may be trying to solve a problem, not knowing that such controlling methods do not produce the desired effects. For example, a parent buys tickets for the whole family to go to a show, without checking other family members' schedules. The parent's motive is to have more time together as a family. If someone resists, the parent says, "Don't you agree that time as a family is important?" Statements that begin, "Don't you agree . . ." are usually mild power strategies.

The next step may be sulking to make the other person feel guilty enough to give in. If "sulk" doesn't work, then "I ain't budging" is the next step. If no one stops it, the escalation continues. The last step is very destructive—beat some sense into the opposition, verbally or physically.

> **Question:** Examine your latest family disagreement. Did any of you sulk? Use guilt? Refuse to listen to the other's feelings? Try to force your way? Control the problem by trying to solve it in your own way, without others' input? Where could you have intervened in the early stages to listen, understand, and come into agreement, so that all felt valued? Decide now what you will do differently to stop the destructive patterns your family has been practicing.

Protection. While attack power strategies are played to win, protection or defense power strategies are used when the person doesn't expect to win. They are also destructive to a loving family, because they try to hurt, rather than build up. At their root, they are forms of revenge. Some defense strategies are sending zingers or inflicting small hurts that aggravate and punish the victor for winning. Other defense strategies are using guilt or retaliation to spoil a winner's victory, "I'll go to the stupid play with the family, but I'll pout and grumble the entire time." Another form of protection or defense is avoidance. A person may be so afraid of conflict that he or she watches TV, reads, works, or plays sports to avoid conflict.

Power struggles. Power strategies do not resolve conflict. They may end an immediate conflict, but families who use control, guilt, revenge, and stubborn refusal to budge, often become locked into serious struggles over who can say how the issue will be resolved. You can tell if you are in a power struggle if you continually rehearse conversations, thinking, "Who does she think she is? I've got rights too."

Remember God's words, "See that none of you repays evil for evil, but always seek to do good to one another and to all" (1 Thess. 5:15 RSV). Persistent valuing love can stop the cycle of hurt. Persistent valuing love cracks the shell of defense and gets to the core of the inner self, where healing can occur. Such persistent love is not mushy, permissive love. Strong love does not allow destructive behaviors to continue. It values, builds up, and encourages as it trains.

> **Suggestion:** If you find yourself and your children in either a cold or an open war, several things can help. When tempers run high, take time out and have everyone, including yourself, write or draw what you're feeling and thinking for 10 minutes. Then make time, no matter how busy you are, to talk.

> **Suggestion:** Persistent valuing is more important than winning power. With persistent valuing, the need to obtain power will eventually collapse. Avoid devaluing. Look for ways to meet both people's needs or interests. Give your children some power and control when possible by asking for their advice and letting them choose among acceptable alternatives.

Question: Look at your relationship with each of your children. Are you devaluing them in words or actions? Are you failing to value them in words or actions? Be honest with yourself. Ask God to show you. Pray, "Search me, O God, and know my heart. Try me and know my thoughts. And see if there be any wicked (devaluing) way in me" (Ps. 139:23–24 RSV).

Work

Another component of Christ's pattern of "faith working through love" is work. Good parenting requires work. The second law of thermodynamics, called the law of entropy, says that everything in the universe will run downhill if left to itself. Energy must be applied to make things improve. In gardening, this is obvious. If you leave your garden unattended, you will grow magnificent weeds but little that's edible.

In human relationships this law of entropy is also true. A good family requires work. Many family problems occur simply because family members are too busy to put in effort to keep chaos at a low roar, or they get discouraged and quit working on their family. Without effort, relationships slide downhill.

We give great energy, in our family, to working at making our home a fun, happy, warm, upbuilding haven. We also put great effort into teaching, building up, kindly correcting, and encouraging the good while punishing the bad, and training our children. The world can be rough. We want our home to not only be a training ground for our children to grow and learn to be godly, but also to be a place where each of us is free to reach God's goals for our lives, because we "encourage one another and build one another up" (1 Thess. 5:11 RSV). Hebrews 10:24–25 tells us to "consider how to stir up one another to love and good works," and to encourage one another. That is our goal. We hope it will be yours.

Faith

Faith Involves Accepting Jesus as Savior, Lord, and Forgiver

Faith working through love originates with God's love, work, and faithfulness.

Jesus is Savior. Faith means, first, that you must accept and receive Christ as your Savior, if you have not already. When you have accepted his death in your place and received his forgiveness for your sins, you are then ready to allow him to pour his love through you to your children. Those who do not have Christ living in them can certainly love their children, but parenthood takes more than human love. You need God's love flowing through you if you're to love and work his way.

Jesus is Lord. Sometimes, you might wish that you could play God in your child's life and fix his or her problems or take away his or her pain. But *playing* God is not the answer. *Relying* on God is.

As much as you'd like to be in control, you are not and cannot be. You are not responsible for your family's healing. God is, and he doesn't want you to try futilely to fix problems by your own power. He wants you to entrust your children into his arms as early as possible, then let them become independent gradually, as you train, encourage, correct, and lift them in prayer to a Father who loves them even more than you do.

When problems arise that your own power can no longer handle, you clearly see your need for solutions that are beyond yourself. You need Jesus as your Lord. As you received, by faith, his death and resurrection to redeem you, you also can receive, by faith, his love to work through you. However, it takes time for God to change, heal, and rid you of attitudes and habits that block his love. If your cup is full of bitterness and unforgiveness, no matter how much living water Christ pours into your cup, bitter water will pour out, until you seek his forgiveness and cleansing.

Question: Do you have faith in Jesus' power and love to transform your life and the lives of your children?

Question: Are you willing for him to use you in his ways in your children's lives?

Jesus is Forgiver. Are you holding onto hurts and refusing to forgive your children because "they don't deserve to be forgiven"? Forgiving them doesn't mean that you let them off the hook, but it allows you to use punishment in love, with the motive of training and not revenge. Unforgiveness and bitterness block the flow of Christ's love to heal those hurts and change you and your children (Ps. 66:18). We *must* forgive (Matt. 6:15; Eph. 4:32). Ask God to help you understand why your children act as they do. That may help you forgive. Ask Him to help you release the hurt to him. He wants to help us carry our burdens (1 Pet. 5:7). He forgives us and sets us free of past hurts.

Suggestion: Close your eyes and visualize Jesus holding out his arms. Then visualize yourself handing your burdens (bitterness, grudges, hurts, unforgiveness, disappointments) to Jesus. Thank him for taking them.

Faith Involves Laying Down Your Life for Your Children

Faith involves (1) acting in love, and (2) trusting God to use the actions for his purposes.

Acting in love. Jesus said that, "Greater love has no man than this, that a man lay down his life for his friends" (John 15:13 RSV). Laying down your life for your spouse, children, or friends may mean giving up your physical life but it also certainly means that you give up your right to always have things your way at your convenience. You may want to read a book or watch a ball game, but you choose to put your child's need for time with you ahead of your own need for time alone. Don't run from the room screaming, "I can't take it. I must have ten minutes—okay, two minutes—alone." This doesn't mean that you will never again get time alone. (It only feels that way sometimes.) But each time you choose to give up what you want or need for your child's sake, you are laying down your life for him or her. Christ says this is an important way to show love.

Choose to "die" to your selfish nature. God can change you without your permission, but it is less painful and usually faster, if you cooperate with the changes. Can you imagine a physician trying to operate to remove a deadly infection while the patient runs half-crazed around the operating room?

Ephesians 4:22, 24 (RSV) tells us to "put off your old nature which belongs to your former manner of life," and "put on the new nature, created after the likeness of God in true righteousness and holiness." Romans 6:6 (RSV) puts the same message another way, "We know that our old self was crucified with him so that the sinful body might be destroyed, and we might no longer be enslaved to sin." God's people are to make a daily choice not to live in the old destructive patterns.

"Dying" to your own desires and putting others first is not popular in this look-out-for-number-one society. Your selfish flesh doesn't like it either. Some friends and "experts" may tell you to do what helps *you* feel good. Your flesh likes that advice. However, the best way to have deep joy and close relationships with your children is to practice love *Christ's* way, not the world's way. It'll be worth it.

Faith in action (more or less). I (Everett) love many sports. Ten years ago, wrestling was not one. Then, first-grade Jonathan burst through the front door shouting, "I want to be a wrestler." Kirby swallowed her bubble gum and went into shock. My eyes glazed, and while I didn't actually drool, I did stutter for a week. Pictures of Jonathan being slammed by some miniature Hulk Hogan rushed through both of our minds.

After being assured that wrestling in the elementary grades had one of the lowest injury rates of any sport and that it was not like TV rastlin', we let Jonathan wrestle. He loved it.

I started calling myself "Bubba," read books on youth wrestling, and assisted knowledgeable coaches for five years so that I could help Jonathan at home and be a part of Jonathan's world. We wrestled together in the living room at night. Kirby would hear, "Let's try this, Daddy. It's called the 'banana split.' I'll just put your left leg here and your right leg way over there and now apply a little pressure. What's that, Daddy? I can't understand you if you're screaming and crying."

Adults don't bend like children, and I woke up many a morning, after nightly practice sessions, looking (and feeling) like a pretzel. Now *that* was laying down my life. It became my joy to give up my time and my own vision of which sports I wanted Jonathan to play to help Jonathan enjoy and succeed at his choice.

Faith Involves Investing in Your Children's Lives

Investing your time, energy, and life in your children may not pay immediate dividends. "Now faith is the assurance of things hoped for, the conviction of things not seen" (Heb. 11:1 RSV). When Christen, our oldest child, was born, we began saving for her college. We put money in long-term accounts to earn interest. Christen is now in college. We had faith in the bank that our money plus interest would be there for college. We did not see our money during those seventeen years of saving. But faith is "the conviction of things not seen." We had enough faith in the bank to invest our money with them.

Surely the Lord of Creation is worthy of even more faith. Banks may fail, but God never fails. Parents can trust him. By investing your time, love, energy, money, and creativity into your children, using God's pattern of valuing and not devaluing them, you know you *will* some day see the dividends—multiplied—even if you don't see the results immediately.

God said, "So shall my word be that goes forth from my mouth; it shall not return to me empty, but it shall accomplish that which I purpose, and prosper in the thing for which I sent it" (Isa. 55:11 RSV). If his Word will accomplish his purpose, then you can believe him when his Word says, "Do not be deceived; God is not mocked, for whatever a man sows, that he will also reap. . . . And let us not grow weary in well-doing, for in due season we shall reap, if we do not lose heart" (Gal. 6:7, 9 RSV). God's Word says that if you "train up a child in the way he should go, . . . when he is old he will not depart from it" (Prov. 22:6 RSV).

Since God said for you to train your children and invest your lives and prayers in them, you can trust that though they may take detours, and though you may make blunders, *God is trustworthy.* "He who began a good work in you (and them) will bring it to completion at the day of Jesus Christ" (Phil. 1:6 RSV). Your faith is not in parenting techniques, though they can be helpful. Your faith is in Almighty God that he will work, and teach you how to work, in the lives of your children.

Question: Have you met Jesus personally? If not, he invites you to allow him to enter your life and give you his life.

Question: Are you allowing Jesus to be Lord and King in your life, or are you trying to keep control? Ask him to show you areas where you have not yet fully surrendered to him.

Activity: List some ways you have put your own desires and needs before your family's. How can you respond differently when needs conflict next time?

Question: Are you making regular deposits of prayer, time together, training, discipline, and valuing love into your child's account?

Faith Working through Love

Faith, work, and love—these three strands make up the thread that holds the family together. Ignore any one of the three and the family can unravel. If your child is having difficulties, then your and your child's faith, work, and love are becoming threadbare. Strive to interweave faith, work, and love, and the family bonds will grow strong.

3

The Solution

Problems in child rearing result from weaknesses in faith working through love by either the child, the parent, or both. The solution to those problems is simple to say, but not to do. Repair failures in faith, work, and love, and live out Christ's pattern in the future. If you do that, you will be following God's discipleship principle. God wants to train you, the parent, in faith, work, and love to make you a stronger disciple of Jesus Christ. God also wants you to pass the discipleship principle to your children—to train them in faith, work, and love to be stronger disciples of Jesus Christ, too.

Activity: Make two posters to remind yourself of your main goals. On one poster, write, "I want to be a better disciple of Jesus Christ and to help my child be a better disciple, too." On the second poster, write, "I want to strengthen my faith, keep working, and exercise valuing love today."

Faith

Jesus showed the way out of the cycle filled with hurt and retaliation. When Jesus willingly gave up his life for us, he redeemed us from the Fall. When we accept him as Savior, he lives within us and we are no longer slaves to sin with no choice. We can choose, with his help, to follow his example and give ourselves for others instead of demanding our way, comfort, and convenience. We may have habits that are so ingrained by years of practice that we react without knowing we have a choice. But we do have a choice and Christ can set us free from captivity to those destructive patterns if we will cooperate and work with him (Ps. 146:7; John 8:36; Gal. 5:1; Isa. 61:1; Luke 4:17–21).

Having children allows parents endless opportunities to sacrifice their own way, learning faith, work, and love in the laboratory of the family. Children are neither comfortable nor convenient for parents; however, children are a blessing and a joy. If parents are willing, God can use the parents to stop destructive family cycles by helping them, through faith, choose love.

Persistent valuing love can stop the cycle of hurt, but persistent valuing love must be applied through faith in Jesus. Hope in Jesus, not in your will power alone.

That doesn't mean you wait passively for Christ to zap you into a perfect parent. (Don't we wish.) To the contrary, work hard to improve your parenting. Don't allow your *motivation* to be self-centered—to ease your own pain or distress or to win approval for being a good parent. You'll want to be a better parent because you love God and want to please him, because you want to bring your life in line with his will by his power.

Activity: Think of a recurring problem in your family that you have been trying to solve on your own. If you haven't yet, invite the Lord to help. Thank God for his answers that will come.

If you have given the problem to God and see no answers yet, ask yourself if you really want *his* answers, or do you want control? He may be waiting for you to be willing to change, or to see if you want change enough to sacrifice some unhealthy pleasures. Ask him to help you want to work his way.

Work

Christian parenting requires work, but effort doesn't have to be drudgery. Make work with your children fun. Ev used to read devotions and stories to each of the children each night before bed. (Now they read even more than he does.) After 50 repetitions of the same stories, it brought laughter when they caught him changing the tales. He made animal noises ("The cat goes 'Moo.'" "No, Daddy, it goes 'Meow.'"), told fairy tales with blatant errors ("Then Little Red Riding Hood pulled a gun and told the wolf, 'Pick flowers yourself, Bucko.'" "No, Daddy, the wolf ran off to Grandma's house"). It taught them to listen, to remember facts, and to enjoy reading.

Work can upbuild the parent as well as the child. When a parent assists with a youth sports team, the parent is able to play with his or her son or daughter, enjoy the outdoors, engage in a sport, help other children in the community, and show the child that the parent cares about him or her. (Want to see Ev's soccer scars?)

People evaluate each other's love for them by monitoring the time and energy they put into the relationship. Effort, time, and energy are far more valuable currencies in the family than is money. While work is needed to maintain or improve a relationship, work alone will have little lasting effect. The work must be done with love and joy for its effects to last.

Question: Is learning fun at your home? Have you set up your child's environment to make learning as creative and joyful as possible? Do you all laugh a lot (but not at each other's expense)? Is there more praise for right attitudes and work attempted than there is nagging for jobs not accomplished? (See Appendixes A, B, and C for fun ways to train.)

Question: Are you taking time to be with each child regularly? Do you wrestle or read, play soccer in the backyard, or draw together? Do you coach a team, help with some activity, cook with a child, go see at least some of your child's performances and games? In this busy society this isn't easy, but it is important "work" that shows love.

Love

Lay Down Your Life

Parents, since you are more mature, take the lead in "laying down your life" for your children. This does not mean that you spoil children by always giving them their way. Rather, listen to them, discern their needs, and try to meet those needs in healthy ways. For example, a brother who is teasing his sister may need attention. Ask him to help you with a project. Then give him positive attention when he is helping you.

Listen

Value your children by listening to them and reflecting back what they said. Reflecting means repeating, paraphrasing, or summarizing their ideas. For example, you might say, "It sounds like you believe I was unfair by getting the tickets without asking your plans, and you're angry. Is that what you're saying?" Show that you are trying to understand. Listening will help you understand their agenda *before* you start giving advice.

Be Sensitive to Their Needs

Watch for signs of impatience and stress in your children. When pressures mount they get stressed out and want to spend less time in relationships. You may sense that a child is pulling back, which may make you ask for more time at the very time the child's stress level is making him or her want less time together. The child isn't rejecting you personally, but it feels that way. Try to see what's behind a sensed rejection, instead of reacting to being hurt with distress, retaliation, or demands.

Avoid Power Strategies and Struggles

Remember our discussion in Chapter 2 about power strategies? If you are trying to reach an agreement with your child and it's not working, do you get louder and more coercive? That will escalate the battle, which neither of you want. What do you really want? Do you want to win and keep the illusion that you are in control, or do you want to train your child into a better disciple of Christ by modeling communication that is Christ-like, thereby building a life-long special relationship?

How do you get out of a power struggle? Do something different. Proverbs 15:1 says, "A soft answer turns away wrath." Softening your voice will calm you and your child. Actively listen. Figure out what your child needs. Does he or she need to be included in family decisions? Does he or she need to know that his or her ideas are valued? Learning to recognize the need behind misbehavior takes effort.

Check out your motives. Ask God to help you recognize when you want control and power and when you want your way because it is truly best for the child's growth. Be honest with yourself. If you discern that you are just wanting power, then help your child speak to you respectfully and choose to let the child win that time. To get out of power struggles, avoid using a hurtful power strategy or becoming involved in a win-at-any-price power struggle. Choose to make your child feel valuable.

Confess

When Jonathan was four years old he left a favorite toy outside. It rained that night and ruined the toy. That would have been a perfect time to show him the toy, hold him and understand his grief at the loss, and then use that to train him to put away his things. But I (Kirby) had had a horrible day. Pressures were high. I was exhausted, and this was the last straw. (Good excuses, huh?) I lost my temper. "Jonathan, what's the matter with you? Will you never learn to put away your things?"

His face fell. His eyes filled with tears, and he said, "I don't know what's the matter with me, Mama." At that moment, I realized what I'd done—I'd given our son the false message that something was wrong with him, and that he'd never learn. I had given him a bad label. I had selfishly reacted to my own frustration born of trying for a long time to train the children to put away their things, and I'd lost my temper. I immediately knelt down close to Jonathan and said, "Jonathan, *nothing* is wrong with you. You did a wrong thing and now your toy is ruined—but you are a wonderful boy and you will learn to put your things away. I'm so sorry that I lost my temper. Can you forgive me?"

"Sure, Mama." Hug, smile.

"I'm sorry that your toy is ruined. Next time what will you do with your toys?"

"I'll put them away."

Confess honestly when you wrong your child and ask forgiveness from him or her. Don't wait for your child to confess and don't confess in the hopes of forcing your child to. Do what Christ commanded (James 5:16): confess to each other that you may be healed. Your children will not lose respect for you if you admit you are wrong. Just the opposite. It takes courage and strength to admit faults and to ask forgiveness. If you want your children to admit when they are wrong, model it first.

Besides modeling confession, train children how to confess. Help them go to those they have hurt to ask forgiveness and help them try to repair the damage when possible.

Confession is risky. It opens a channel into your inner core, where you are vulnerable. That is threatening because you may find out, and even worse, others may find out, that you are not perfect. It costs something to admit being wrong. When you confess to your children, they too know the cost, and it tells them they are worth a great price that you are willing to pay that price to have a great relationship with them.

If you hurt your children but refuse to confess and ask their forgiveness, they may assume that you don't care or that you don't value them, which adds other wounds to the existing wound. Healing requires vulnerability, confession, and a willingness to change.

Put Your Love to Work

After you have confessed your hurtful actions to your children and have asked their forgiveness, tell them that you'll need their help to change. Ask them to pray with you regularly for God's help to change you. If they have been wounded often they may mistrust you at first, but keep trying. They will respond as you consistently value and build them up.

> **Activity:** Examine your heart before the Lord. Have you hurt your child and not dealt with it? It takes humility and courage to admit you are wrong. God will help you if you ask him. Don't excuse your behavior. Don't tell the child how wrong he or she was. Tell your child what you did that was wrong and humbly ask forgiveness. If it helps you, take the time now to write out what you want to say. Then do it.

Practice Faith Working through Love

Practicing faith working through love is a discipline. It is the constant work of a disciple of Jesus Christ. Faith working through love is a general strategy through which you should filter each decision. It is not unlike Charles Sheldon's classic novel, *In His Steps*, in which people decide to pause before each decision and ask, "What would Jesus do?"

Because faith working through love is a discipleship strategy, not a technique, we cannot possibly illustrate its use in all of the cases in which you'll employ it. We want it to be more than "theory," though, so we have chosen some illustrations, and we offer practical principles for parenting and application to some more serious problems in later chapters.

Don't Discourage; Encourage Your Children

Hurtful words *dis*courage, but helpful words *en*courage. Encouragement puts courage to try *into* us. Words that build up and point out a child's improvements put courage in him or her not to give up, but to keep trying. Hurtful words *discourage*. Such words can drain a child of courage to change. Practice faith working through love by encouraging your child.

The Bible teaches not to discourage. "Do not let any unwholesome talk come out of your mouths, but only what is helpful for building others up according to their needs, that it may benefit those who listen.... Get rid of all bitterness, rage and anger, brawling and slander, along with every form of malice. Be kind and compassionate to one another, forgiving each other, just as in Christ God forgave you" (Eph. 4:29, 31, 32 NIV). Parents can drain courage from a child by put downs, sarcasm, or belittling jokes or comments. Avoid these.

The Bible teaches parents to encourage. It says, "Therefore encourage one another and build one another up.... Admonish the idlers, encourage the fainthearted, help the weak, be patient with them all. See that none of you repays evil for evil, but always seek to do good to one another and to all" (1 Thess. 5:11, 14, 15). It also says, "Be humble and gentle. Be patient with each other, making allowance for each other's faults because of your love. Try to be led along together by the Holy Spirit, and so be at peace with one another" (Eph. 4:2, 3 LB).

With God's help, you can change habits of communication from belittling to encouraging. If you ask your Heavenly Father to help you do his will, he won't turn you down. We have assurance, "And this is the confidence we have in him, that if we ask anything according to his will he hears us. And if we know that he hears us in whatever we ask, we know that we have obtained the requests made of him" (1 John 5:14–16 RSV). "Whatever you ask in my name, I will do it, that the Father may be glorified in the son; if you ask anything in my name, I will do it" (John 14:13, 14 RSV). "You do not have, because you do not ask" (James 4:2 RSV). Ask him to help you change the way you speak to your children. He will.

Don't Devalue; Value Your Children

Practice faith working through love by valuing your child. If something is valuable, you are willing to give something you value for it. For example, if you see a book you really want or need, you are willing to give money for that book. You value the book more than you value the money it costs. The same thing is true if you choose to show your children that you value them. You give something of value for them.

What of value can you give your children? It might be your time, willingness to communicate, efforts to get to know them, energy to do creative and fun things together, money to help meet their needs and sometimes to help them reach their dreams, affections and hugs, and words that build them up. Giving money without time and affection is not enough. Give as much time and love as you can.

> **Question:** List what is of value to you. What items on that list can you share with your family to help them feel that you value them?

Activity: Each family member may want to be shown love differently. List at least two ways you can show love to each family member. If you are unsure, ask, "How can I show you love in a way that you can receive?"

Don't Tease; Enjoy Your Children

Practice faith working through love by enjoying your child without teasing. If children have heard clear, genuine compliments and valuing words (and they trust that the source is sincere), they will usually prefer those forms of affection and encouragement to teasing. If your family has developed the habit of putdown teasing, replace it with kinder and less destructive methods of showing affection. Humor at a person's expense is too expensive. It destroys self-esteem.

Don't Be Sarcastic;
Be Genuine with Your Children

Practice faith working through love by being genuine with your child. Avoid sarcasm. Sarcasm makes children build walls of protection until they refuse to let you in and are unable to show or even recognize their feelings. They fear being vulnerable because they do not trust that you won't later tease them or put them down for their admitted weaknesses. People only share their treasured thoughts with those they trust.

Make sure nonverbal messages agree with verbal messages. If you need to correct your child, speak to the wrong action, and don't give devaluing looks. Say, "I really don't like it when you run screaming through the house. I love you. But please leave noisy play outside. Thank you." If your children have done something wrong, it is kinder and more effective to tell them clearly and gently exactly what they did rather than hope they pick it up from sarcasm, jokes, sighs, or looks. "The look" may temporarily stop bad behavior, but it gives the wrong message. It says, to the child's mind, "You're bad. I disapprove of you." That is not the message you want to get across. Ask God to help you replace those hurtful communication forms with more effective ones.

Faith, Work, and Love

The solution to problems in Christian living—and thus in Christian parenting—is to have a godly blueprint and build from it consistently. To apply faith working through love consistently, parents need a vision of what the family can be.

4

A Christian Vision
of Parenting

Mary, a single mother, stumbles in the door, baby Tim under one arm and Jerry, two, clinging to her right ankle. The groceries are under the other arm, and the diaper bag is between her teeth. Mary wants to plop in a chair, put up her tired feet, and stare (drooling) at the wall for an hour or two. But Tim's aromatic dirty diaper and Jerry's wail thwart her escape plans. She staggers to her feet, ready to run away screaming, but whispers a prayer instead. She knows she has a choice.

Choose What to Focus Your Vision On

The Bible provides us a vision of the family as people who are committed to each other, who sacrifice their own wants and rights for the good of other family members, who strive to be Christ-like as they disciple each other, and who practice faith working through love. Mary can choose to focus on herself or her children. Mary knows that if she puts her children's needs first, she can trust God to meet her needs. She wants to practice Philippians 2:3, which says, "Do nothing out of selfish ambition or vain conceit, but in humility consider others better than yourselves" (NIV).

Vision Requires Planning

Mary also knows she needs to have a game plan if she is to meet her children's needs effectively despite all she has to do. With children of any age, little is accomplished without planning.

During the times (rare, you may say) when you have energy, arrange your home for the times when you know you will be exhausted. In the evening or the morning, whatever works for you, make the time to set up learning games and activities for later. Keep a file of activities that are fun and are appropriate for your children's ages. Then prepare a few activities for easy access when you need them. Don't wait to be creative when you are exhausted and the children are screaming. Few can pull that off. Don't try to be creative on your own. Ask friends, librarians, and teachers for ideas. Read books. Gather ideas from many sources, change the ideas to fit your situation and, voila, a learning game is born.

Let's look again at Mary, as she staggers into the house with babies and groceries. This time she is ready. The night before she set up a bouncing seat for baby Tim and placed a cake pan on a towel under the seat. Today, she enters mumbling to herself. She quickly changes Tim's diaper (remember the aroma) and places him in the bouncing chair. She pours warm water in the pan. His bare feet splash and kick delightedly. He is fascinated and happy. (NOTE: Recent studies have shown that some types of bouncing seats are not safe. Avoid those, and never leave a baby unattended in one.)

Also the previous night, Mary had prepared a surprise for two-year-old Jerry. She placed a can of shaving cream on a dark plastic place mat and put a towel nearby. On the way home, Mary had told Jerry that she had a game for him to play when they got home. When they arrive, Mary squirts shaving cream on the dark surface, then demonstrates how to spread the shaving cream smoothly and how to draw pictures using fingers and hands. She also shows Jerry how he can "erase" the picture and draw another. He finger paints while she encourages his efforts, helps the baby, and fixes dinner. When Jerry is through, Mary helps him wipe up the soap with the cloth and rinse his hands. (P.S., he doesn't have to wash his hands before dinner. Good deal.)

When parents meet their children's needs *first*, there is joy, not frustration. The parent's need for peace is met by putting the children's needs first. God's ways are good.

> **Activity:** Think up two activities that your child (or each child if you have more than one) would enjoy. Prepare the materials for those activities so that the next time you feel harried, you already have an activity prepared.

Provide a Clear Vision of the Rules

Children need a clear vision of the rules so that they know what you expect. Rules provide limits. Children need limits to feel secure. One example of this has been told for so long that the original source has been lost. On a playground surrounded by a chain link fence, children played with joy. Once day the fence was torn down, and afterwards the teachers noticed a dramatic change in the children's play. Children no longer played on all of the equipment. They played only on the equipment in the center of the playground. Limits do not take away children's freedom to learn. To the contrary, limits add security and build self-confidence which gives more freedom to explore and learn within the limits.

Children need to know clearly what is expected of them. Imagine yourself on a job. The boss tells you that he or she expects you to do your job well. Great. You want to do well.

Your boss says, "Put the wackets into the duflinger on the north fratchet of the scrubup."

"Say what?" you say, asking the boss to explain.

But the boss yells at you, "Hurry and do it. Are you lazy?"

You try to do what was asked only to be scolded repeatedly. "What's the matter, stupid? Can't you do anything right?"

Over time, by trial and error, you might hit upon what's expected of you, but your self-esteem by then will probably be lower than a grasshopper's belly. How much nicer if the boss had clearly explained what was expected, let you ask questions, and demonstrated what was required. There would have been less chance of failure and more opportunity for praising your successes.

When children misbehave, often you have not provided a clear vision of your expectations for their behavior or for the consequences of their obedience or disobedience. When children misbehave, (1) reflect on the way you communicated what you expected, (2) assess the child's reaction to determine what need the child is trying to meet, (3) devise a strategy to meet the need, and (4) clearly explain your expectations.

Reflect on how you communicated what you expected. You knew what you wanted the child to do. The child should know, too. Right? Did you communicate clearly? Be honest with yourself. Check to see if the rules for behavior are right for the child's age and abilities. Ask yourself the following questions: "Are the rules beyond my child's maturity?" "Are the rules consistent, or do I reward one time, ignore the next, and punish the next, because I have a headache?" "Does my child know what I expect and can he or she do it?"

Assess the child's reaction. When children misbehave, they are usually trying to meet a need but doing so ineffectively. Assess your child's behavior and what it may mean. To get his or her needs met (see the parentheses following), the child may become

- clingy and shy (trying to get comfort),
- rebellious (trying to get respect),
- aggressive (trying to gain control or power),
- perfectionistic (trying to gain approval),
- loud (trying to get understanding of how he or she feels),
- obnoxious (trying to get needed attention),
- conceited (trying to get a sense of competence and worth).

Devise a strategy to meet your child's needs. If the child is clinging for comfort, give extra comfort for good behavior. If the child is rebelling to gain respect, catch the child doing good things and tell him or her how much you admire the child. The principle is the same for each need. Look for opportunities to provide for the child's needs and do so when the child is behaving well, not misbehaving.

Clearly explain your expectations. Think about how your child might interpret what you say. State the rule clearly and tell the child what will happen if he or she obeys and disobeys.

Activity: Examine each behavior listed above (e.g., clingy and shy, rebellious, etc.). If your child shows any of those behaviors, ask yourself whether you are meeting the child's needs. If not, plan at least three things you can do (when the child is behaving well) to meet the child's needs and short-circuit misbehavior.

Involve children. Be sure that older children have a say in setting the rules. After children are age seven, they should be involved in making the rules (in small ways at first). The need to have input on family rules peaks in adolescence. By listening to your child's opinion, you help give him or her a sense of control and you tell your child that you value his or her feelings and ideas.

You Need a Vision
of What Parenting Style to Choose

Diana Baumrind (1967; 1971) pioneered research that compared three parenting styles. *Authoritarian* parents set laws that were not to be questioned. They punished every misconduct. Parents were aloof and rarely showed affection or approval. Their family was a dictatorship. Some Christian parents believe that this is what the Bible teaches. They accept verses like Proverbs 13:24 about using the rod but overlook verses about encouragement, gentleness, and affection (Prov. 19:18; Prov. 15:1; Eph. 4:29).

Permissive parents made few demands of the children and tried to hide their impatience when children misbehaved. Rules were set but not enforced. Permissive parents were noncontrolling and allowed children to regulate their own behavior. Permissive parents were low on control but high on support and affection. Anarchy usually reigned in the home.

Authoritative parents set limits and enforced rules but were willing to listen to the child's requests and questions. The home was more democratic than dictatorial, with parent leadership. Love, support, and affection as well as limits and control were high.

Research found that authoritative parents (high affection *and* control) produced the most self-reliant, self-controlled, content, friendly, cooperative, and high-achieving children (Baumrind 1967, 1971). Children of authoritative parents also were often successful, happy with themselves, and generous with others as they got older (Berger 1988). Children raised by permissive parents were the least self-controlled, the least self-reliant, and most *unhappy* (Baumrind 1967, 1971). While, as a group, the daughters did well in school, the sons of permissive parents were low-achievers. Other research found the permissively raised children to be aggressive (Berger 1988). Authoritarian (dictatorial) parenting produced distrustful, unhappy, hostile sons, and poorly achieving children of both sexes (Baumrind 1967, 1971).

If you know what kind of children you want yours to be, choose your parenting style accordingly. Have *faith* in God's Word when he says that discipline and training in righteousness, as well as valuing love and encouragement, are all essential parts of God's plan for raising children. Understand that effective parenting takes *work*, lots of it, but it is worth the effort. Apply *love*, valuing love, at every opportunity.

We love it when secular research shows what God said all along. What a wonderful Lord! Together, Scripture and research say that consistent, loving discipline, and valuing, affectionate, supportive love are both essential in raising children who will be prepared to be what God intended them to be.

Refocusing Blurred Vision

If you have, until now, been inconsistent or lax with your discipline (the permissive style), you may now be reaping the fruits of unhappy, self-centered, unself-disciplined children who act out their unhappiness in demanding and unpleasant ways. If your child is young, begin now to set clear rules and train your child to follow them. If your child is entering the teen years, this is *not* the time suddenly to enforce new rules on a teen who has never been taught to obey. That would be like trying to put out a kitchen fire using paint thinner. Ka-boom! Instead, tell a teen, "I'm sorry that I didn't teach you, when you were younger, the importance of following rules. I've just found out that the Bible tells parents to discipline their children, and I didn't. Please forgive me for not following God's plan better." (At this point the child's eyes roll, and the hair bristles.) So you say, "Don't worry. I'm not going to impose a lot of arbitrary rules on you now." (The child thinks, "Hot dog! Chaos as usual!") You continue, "But I do plan to try to be closer to what God wants, and I need your help." (Ears perk up.) "I would like for us, *together*, to try to solve the problems we are having. I love you and I can see that your current path will probably lead you into future pain. I want joy for you and not pain." *Together* decide on reasonable rules and rewards your child can work toward when the rules are kept (and fair punishments if the rules are broken).

Then comes the real work. If the teen is not used to following rules, he or she will test you. *Before* he or she breaks a rule, praise good actions or attitudes. Tell the teen how excited you are about both of you making an effort to love each other. But follow through with the plan. Be consistent with punishment the teen has agreed upon. "Remember, this is what you decided was fair. You need to accept the punishment we decided upon together. I hope there won't be a need for punishment again." You can ask the teen to choose an alternative punishment, if you agree it is equivalent, but be sure not to slip back into permissiveness when the going gets tough.

If you have been authoritarian (dictatorial) up to now, explain to your children that you mistakenly thought that was God's plan. Tell the children that you now know that you were wrong. Ask forgiveness. Begin showing affection and sincerely praise your child's efforts. After your child trusts your sincerity, he or she will respond. Be diligent in praise. Involve the child in choosing which rules are fair and good and which, if any, are too harsh. Often the child doesn't mind the rules. He or she just wants you to value his or her opinion and to listen and understand.

A Positive Vision of Discipline

Many hear the word "discipline" and immediately think "punishment." But from now on, when you hear "discipline," think "disciple-making." Discipline is more than punishment.

It is training in righteousness, training in right behaviors and attitudes. Discipline is training disciples of Jesus.

How can you do that? Jesus did not make disciples by constant rebuke. He taught and encouraged far more than he chastised. As you think about the way Jesus made disciples, you learn that good discipline does not *just* involve punishment for wrong. Even more often it should include instruction, training, praise, and encouragement for good behaviors and attitudes.

Hey world! We heard Bud Halzie speak at a conference. He spoke about his "Hey world" philosophy. When his children did any behavior that showed good character and responsibility by choosing to do right or any time they worked hard toward a goal, he yelled out for the world to hear, "Hey world! Sara worked hard and made honor roll. That takes character!" "Hey world! Sam washed the clothes without being asked. What a kind man he's becoming!"

Children want attention and approval. Some sensitive children may get embarrassed if you roll down the car window and shout so all can hear. Others love it. Either way, let the child know with flourish that you noticed his or her effort. "Hey world!"

Don't brag about talent—brag about action. Talent is a gift from God. We want to be grateful for God's gifts, but encourage the hard work to use and improve the gift to bring God glory.

Not too long ago, after years of "Hey-world" encouraging our children, I (Kirby) told the children something I had done to try to bless their day. Spontaneously, Becca and Katy Anna ran to the front door, opened it and yelled out, "Hey world!"

Question: Do you frequently praise good attitudes and behaviors, or are you more often negative and disapproving? Examine Scripture. Read Table 4–1.

Table 4–1
Some Scripture (NIV) on Discipline:
Punishment and Instruction

Punishment

Psalm 89:30–33   "If his sons forsake my law . . . and fail to keep my commandments, I will *punish* their sin with the rod, their iniquity with flogging; but I will not take my love from him, (*but I will not remove from him my steadfast love* [RSV]) nor will I ever betray my faithfulness" (emphasis mine).

Psalm 119:67   "Before I was afflicted I went astray, but now I obey your word."

Psalm 119:71   "It was good for me to be afflicted so that I might learn your decrees."

Proverbs 13:24   "He who spares the rod hates his son, but he who loves him is careful (diligent [RSV]) to discipline him."

Proverbs 19:18   "Discipline your son, for in that there is hope; do not be a willing party to his death." "Discipline your son while there is hope, but do not indulge your angry resentments by undue chastisements and set yourself to his ruin" (Amplified Bible).

Proverbs 22:15   "Folly is bound up in the heart of a child, but the rod of discipline will drive it far from him."

Proverbs 23:13   "Do not withhold discipline from a child."

Proverbs 29:15   "The rod of correction imparts wisdom, but a child left to himself disgraces (brings shame to—RSV) his mother."

Proverbs 29:17   "Discipline your son, and he will give you peace; he will bring delight to your soul."

Proverbs 29:19   "A servant cannot be corrected by mere words; though he understands, he will not respond."

Lamentations 3:27   "It is good for a man to bear the yoke (be under discipline—LB) while he is young."

John 15:2   "Every branch that does bear fruit he (God) trims clean (*prunes*—RSV) so that it will be even more fruitful."

Hebrews 12:5–11   (quoting from Prov. 3:11–12) "'My son, do not make light of the Lord's discipline, and do not lose heart when he rebukes you, because the LORD disciplines those he loves, and he punishes every one he accepts as a son. . . .' we have all had human fathers to discipline us and we respected them for it. How much more should we submit to the Father of our spirits and live! . . . God disciplines us for our good, that we may share his holiness. No discipline seems pleasant at the time, but painful. Later on, however, it produces a harvest of righteousness and peace for those who have been trained by it."

Instruction

Deuteronomy 11:18–22	"Teach them (God's ways) to your children, talking about them when you sit . . . when you walk . . . when you lie down . . . get up . . . carefully observe all these commands."
Proverbs 13:1	"A wise son heeds his father's instruction."
Proverbs 15:1	"A soft answer turns away wrath, but a harsh word stirs up anger." (Instruction should be kind, loving, and patient, not harsh.)
Proverbs 15:4	"A gentle tongue, with its healing power is a tree of life." (Instruct with gentleness.)
Proverbs 16:24	"Pleasant words are a honeycomb, sweet to the soul and healing to the bones."
Proverbs 22:6	"Train a child in the way he should go, and when he is old he will not turn from it."
Ephesians 4:29	"Do not let any unwholesome talk come out of your mouths, but only what is helpful for building others up according to their needs, that it may benefit those who listen."
Ephesians 4:32	"Be kind and compassionate to one another, forgiving each other, just as in Christ God forgave you."
Ephesians 6:4	"Fathers do not exasperate your children (provoke your children to anger—RSV); instead, bring them up in the training and instruction of the Lord."
1 Thessalonians 5:11	"Therefore encourage one another and build each other up."
2 Timothy 2:24–26	"And the Lord's servant must not quarrel;

> instead, he must be kind to everyone (including children), able to teach, not resentful. Those who oppose him he must gently instruct, in the hope that God will grant them repentance leading them to a knowledge of the truth, and that they will come to their senses and escape from the trap of the devil, who has taken them captive to do his will."

Punishment. Through Scripture, God corrects and punishes, *and* he also teaches, trains, encourages, edifies, and rewards. Here are some guidelines for punishing and for training. When you *punish*, make sure the punishment

- fits the offense,
- is clearly associated, by the child, with the problem (have the child tell you what he or she did wrong),
- is unpleasant (but not harmful) so the child will want to stop the wrong behavior,
- is administered immediately (or as soon as possible),
- is consistently given when deserved,
- is not done in anger,
- is done in love with a desire to train, not done out of revenge,
- is followed by correcting bad behaviors and letting the child know what good actions to choose next time.

For one example of how to punish effectively, see Table 4–2.

Table 4–2
How to Punish without Being Harsh or Abusive

1. Be sure the child understands what *action* he or she did wrong. Ask, "Why are you being punished?" You want the

answer, "because I disobeyed (or whatever the child did)," *not* "because I'm bad." If the child says "I was bad," say, "You are not bad. You are special, and we love you. What you *did* was bad. What did you do wrong?" If the child doesn't know, tell him or her. Ask again until he or she can tell you.

2. Say, "I love you too much to let you keep doing this (name specifically what wrong was done). We need to help you learn not to do (name it) again."

3. Administer the punishment. If you spank, never spank hard enough to leave welts or break the skin. Punishment should *never* do damage. If you impose a restriction, give a clear statement of the limits and time. If you require restitution, make sure the child knows exactly what to do.

4. After the punishment, again ask the child, "Why did you have to be punished?" Be sure he or she understands what was wrong.

5. Have the child apologize and ask forgiveness of whomever he or she wronged, and also of God.

6. Assure the child of God's and of your love and forgiveness. "I love you even when you do wrong things. I want to help you do right. I will always love you."

7. Ask the child what he or she will choose to do next time. Be certain that the child knows what right behavior is expected.

8. Hug. If the child refuses affection, something still needs to be dealt with. The child may still not understand, or may not feel forgiven. The child may feel you've been unfair. Ask the child to tell you what is wrong. "Do you know that I forgive you?" "Are you angry with yourself? With me?" "Do you know I still love you?" If the child is sorry and feels forgiven, he or she will want your affection. Let the child know that he or she is accepted and loved. If the child still sulks, do not give further attention for pouting. Give a time out until he or she is either ready to truly repent, to talk, or to hug and go on with joy. The fruit of true repentance is joy.

Training. When you train, make sure you:

- make eye contact,
- spend time, giving the child your undivided attention,
- make learning fun (using games that train, such as "Come Running When Mama Calls Game," or "The Follow Directions Game"; See Appendixes),

- encourage small steps in the right direction,
- praise good behaviors,
- set up the environment for positive experiences (making games before you're exhausted, child-proofing your home so there is less need for "no-no"),
- avoid packing too much into one day,
- teach when the child is rested, fed, well, and happy,
- set clear, specific rules and consequences,
- have the child repeat the rule, *before* each activity where the rule is needed (For example, before you take your child into the store ask, "What are our rules for the grocery store?" See Appendix E for ideas.),
- give clear warnings before changing activities (i.e., "You may slide two more times and then we must go"),
- teach the child to communicate feelings and needs with respect,
- model kindness, respect and valuing love as well as teaching them.

Summary

A Christian vision for parenting is parent as disciple-maker. As you teach the discipleship principle of faith working through love, you'll also learn to be a better disciple of Jesus yourself. Applying faith working through love will yield a positive vision for parenting:

- putting your child's needs first by planning ahead,
- setting and following clear rules for behavior,
- choosing an authoritative parenting style, which is characterized by high support and firm control, and
- seeing parenting as disciple-making, which uses encouragement, praise, correction, and teaching.

5

Dealing with
Your Child's Problems

As we've described, parenting problems involve weaknesses in implementing the discipleship principle of faith working through love. Christ's principle of faith working through love stresses the importance of trusting God, persisting at working energetically, and valuing and building up children and not devaluing them. Though all problems involve weaknesses in faith, work, and love, many problems major in one weakness more than others. For example, many parenting problems major in weaknesses in love—how to best value and avoid devaluing your child. Some parenting problems involve weaknesses in faith that (a) the Lord can and will work sovereignly in the problem, and (b) if you try to value more and devalue less, then positive things will (over time) happen. Further, parenting problems often worsen when parents give up and stop working, and they cannot be solved without effort, work, a labor of love.

Just as different problems major in weaknesses in faith, work, or love, so also the solutions major in one more than another. For example, the solution to teen rebellion, in one case, may call for more valuing love, finding what needs are not being met, listening, understanding, and working together to meet those needs. In another case, adhering to firm limits (which the teen helped to decide upon), majoring in work, may be the answer. Both solutions involve nurturing and firm love. Both require work and faith, but the emphasis is different.

Agape

Apply AGAPE, God's selfless, wise love, to problems. We have used the acrostic A-G-A-P-E to describe five steps you can take to solve specific parenting problems.

Step 1: Assess

Assess your child's problem and what you can do about it by answering these questions:

- "If I look through the glasses of faith working through love, what new light will I see? Practically, how can I help my child build faith, work, and love, and solve this problem?" Remember, your goals are to make yourself and your child better disciples of Christ, not just put out fires as they arise.
- "Are unmet underlying needs at the root of this current problem?" (See page 53 and Table 5–2, page 79.)

Step 2: Goal Planning

Plan specific actions by answering these questions.

- "How can I value my child more?"
- "How can I avoid devaluing him or her?"
- "How can I help my child be more like Christ through this problem?"
- "How can I help my child meet his or her needs in more acceptable ways?"

- "How can I show more faith through this ordeal?"

Step 3: Action

- Put into action what you planned in Steps 1 and 2. Expect ups and downs. Keep faith and keep working.

Step 4: Persevere

If you feel discouraged, ask yourself:

- "Have I worked enough? Am I quitting too easily?"

Step 5: Evaluate

After you have taken action and persevered, evaluate what happened.

- If what you tried was *not* successful, ask, "How *else* can I value my child in a way he or she can receive? How else can I avoid devaluing? What needs might I have missed?"
- If what you tried was successful, ask, "Have I become a better disciple of Jesus through this? How? How has my child gained in faith, work, and love?"

We now analyze some examples of how to apply faith working through love, using AGAPE. We have divided the problems by their area of greatest weakness. Then we applied AGAPE to find the solution. You certainly won't encounter most of these problems, but by reading through each one, you'll understand better how to analyze problems and solve them through AGAPE. Thus, you'll be better equipped to deal with whatever problems you encounter.

One word of warning is needed. If your child's behavior becomes extreme, if problems persist, or if you have doubts about the seriousness of your child's problem, consult a physician or psychologist about your child. Even if your child can benefit from professional consultation, you can still use the ideas in this chapter to help.

Weaknesses in Faith

Fear

Normal fears. When our oldest daughter, Christen, was around two years old, we were hiking in the woods. We came to a small wooden bridge over a creek. Christen stopped abruptly and wouldn't budge. Panic. As we asked what was wrong, she cried, "I'll fall through the holes." Planks were separated by quarter-inch gaps. To adults that's silly. To a toddler, who has no concept of relative size, it's terrifying. Children may also fear being sucked down the drain after their bath, or into a vacuum cleaner.

Fear is a normal emotional reaction to perceived danger. God gave fear for our protection. For example, it is good if toddlers are afraid at the top of tall stairs, so they don't try to leap down them. Fear of falling is protective. Fears are part of growing up, and certain fears actually show that the brain is developing normally.

Here's an example. Lizzie was a new grandmother who lived three states away from her daughter and couldn't visit often. When Lizzie visited Sammy at five months, Lizzie picked him up to coos and delight. When Sammy was ten months, though, he screeched when Lizzie came near and clung to his mother for dear life. This is normal development. Lizzie was a stranger to Sammy.

The fear of strangers emerges at approximately the same time in every culture (from 6 to 8 months of age), peaks around 14 to 15 months, then subsides and usually disappears by 18 to 24 months. It shows that the baby can remember his or her parents and others whom the baby sees frequently and can distinguish the difference between familiar and new faces.

A similar fear, during approximately the same ages, is separation anxiety—the fear of being left by the parent. This normal fear indicates that the baby realizes that missing objects (such as parents who aren't present) still exist. This is why the nursery for older infants and toddlers usually has heart-wrenching scenes as parents leave their children.

Temperament and experience can affect how long stranger wariness and separation anxiety persist. Shy children or slow-to-warm-up children may be slower to lose these fears. Also, if parents give undue attention to the fear, then the fear can linger. By undue attention, we mean returning to the nursery when the child cries instead of letting the nursery worker calm the child, or staying in the nursery instead of leaving quickly. Separation anxiety is lessened if the parent leaves the child in the nursery quickly and does not linger (Berk 1993).

Some people dwell on fears, worries, and anxieties. Often such habits are learned from childhood. It is not a sin to be afraid, but Jesus told people that when they are afraid and anxious, they are to cast their anxieties on him (1 Pet. 5:7). This takes practice and patience to train ourselves and our children to lift fears to our Lord every time fearful thoughts intrude. We need the persistent love and help of family members and friends to practice such faith. If your child tends to be fearful, see Table 5–1 for some Scriptures that may help build faith. Faith comes from hearing God's Word and from getting to know the One in whom we are trusting.

Table 5–1
Some Bible Verses
Concerning Fear and Trust of God

Isaiah 12:2	(NIV) "I will trust and not be afraid."
Matthew 11:28, 29	(NIV) "Come to me, all you who are weary and burdened, and I will give you rest. Take my yoke upon you and learn from me, for I am gentle and humble in heart, and you

68   Value Your Children

	will find rest for your souls. For my yoke is easy and my burden is light."
1 Peter 5:7	(NIV) "Cast all your anxiety (worries, fears) on him (Jesus) because he cares for you."
Isaiah 43:1, 5	(NIV) "Fear not, for I have redeemed you; I have called you by name; you are mine. . . . Do not be afraid, for I am with you."
Isaiah 7:4	(NIV) "Be careful, keep calm and don't be afraid."
Ezekiel 3:9	(LB) "I have made your forehead as hard as rock. So don't be afraid of them, or fear their sullen, angry looks, even though they are such rebels."
Joel 2:21	(NIV) "Be not afraid, O land; be glad and rejoice, surely the LORD has done great things."
Zechariah 8:13b, 15	(NIV) "Do not be afraid, (or discouraged [LB]) but let your hands be strong."
2 Timothy 1:7	(NIV) "For God did not give us a spirit of timidity (fear), but a spirit of power, of love and of self-discipline."
Hebrews 13:6	(NIV) "The LORD is my helper; I will not be afraid. What can man do to me?"
1 John 4:18	(NIV) "There is no fear in love. But perfect love drives out fear."
Deuteronomy 7:9	(NIV) "The LORD your God is God; he is the faithful God, keeping his covenant of love to a thousand generations of those who love him and keep his commands."

Non-normal fears. Separation anxiety can last longer than normal and become extreme if parents give too much attention to it or if there is poor maternal attachment. Maternal attachment is an infant's feeling of security in the mother's love and availability. Both early or poor day-care experiences (Belsky and Rovine 1985) and unresponsive parenting (not much affectionate contact or loving words) may contribute to poor attachment to parents (Ainsworth et al. 1978; Belsky 1988; Bowlby 1969). Babies need to be cuddled, held, talked to, read to, played with, and delighted in—in short, valued. If babies don't receive such valuing attention, they may become insecure and fearful or hostile, or have adjustment difficulties (Bates and Bayles 1988). Many day-care workers and busy parents are so rushed that they don't meet this emotional need of infants. Children who are poorly attached find it hard to explore and learn, and they find making friends difficult.

Ray and Jodie both held management positions. Jodie loved her job. When Bart was born, Jodie took a leave of absence for six weeks, and then she returned to work. Ray and Jodie loved Bart, so they searched diligently for high-quality day care. The day care they found looked good when they visited the center, but it was inadequate. Overworked child-care employees didn't spend much time with the children. By Bart's third year he was fearful, shy, and easily intimidated. Bart had no sense of stable support because his career-directed, overworked parents were exhausted and had little time for Bart at the end of their busy days. Neither did the day-care professionals. For Bart, the future was bleak. We talked with Ray and Jodie about taking a leave of absence and giving Bart the nurturing he needed, but they loved their work, their house, and the money, and had convinced themselves that Bart would outgrow his insecurities.

A different friend, Charlene, was on the brink of divorce when she became pregnant with Jean. Charlene's husband, Paul, convinced her that if she left him, she could not have custody of Jean. Anticipating divorce, Charlene tried not to get too attached to Jean. Charlene thought that if Jean wasn't close to her, then it wouldn't hurt Jean as much if she left. By age eighteen months, whenever Charlene tried to leave Jean in day care to go to work, Jean became hysterical and cried all day. Jean was terrified to be out of sight of her mother, because she couldn't trust that her mother would return. Jean didn't feel secure in her mother's love.

I (Kirby) talked with Charlene about how positive maternal attachment in infancy and toddlerhood is essential for a

child to make friendships, learn, explore, and be consider-
ate of others as he or she grows older (Bradley et al. 1988).
After Charlene understood what was at stake, she regularly
cuddled Jean and helped her feel secure in her mother's love.
Charlene quit her job, tightened belts, and spent time playing with, teaching, and loving Jean. By the time Jean was
three, Jean's attachment was healthy and secure.

We don't share these examples to make single mothers
feel guilty, or to say that all child care outside the home is
bad. We merely want to challenge you to ask God for other
creative answers to meeting the family's needs and also to
meeting your children's deep need for nurturance, time, and
valuing love. God has answers. Parents may have to give
up some "wants" to meet their children's needs.

Question: Consider what sacrifices you need to make to
help your child develop.

Question: A child learns to have faith in a loving heavenly
Father by first learning to trust his or her earthly parents'
love and care. Do you have regular times (long and short)
set aside on your calendar for your children for activities
such as hobbies, picnics, camping, vacations, reading a
book aloud, walking and talking, devotions, or prayer? Have
you taken time recently for a spontaneous activity with your
children, such as going on a hike, playing ball or a board
game, or spitting watermelon seeds in the yard?

Another type of non-normal fear is called a *phobia*. When
our third child, Becca, was in elementary school she was
selling Girl Scout cookies with her older sister, Christen.
Suddenly, a large dog burst from a door, passed Christen,
and bit Becca. That event was traumatic enough to turn a
normal fear of vicious dogs into an irrational fear of all dogs.

Phobias are irrational specific fears, far out of proportion to the things that trigger them. Becca's fear was not
out of proportion to the dog attack, but after the attack,

Becca would turn pale at the sight of a friendly dog a block away. Some phobias may result from a bad experience, such as in Becca's case. The cause of other phobias is unknown, such as a height phobia in someone who has never fallen (American Psychiatric Association 1994).

Let's use phobias to show AGAPE at work. First, *Assess.* Suppose your child is fearful of dogs, like Becca was. Look at the problem through the glasses of faith working through love. What do you see? Fear majors in a weakness in faith and minors in weaknesses in work and love. The child's faith in the Lord's ability or willingness to protect him or her is low. Your child's and your faith in God's love, that God really means good for your child's life may be shaken (Jer. 29:11). Reestablishing trust is needed. Work is needed to get over abnormal fears. Nurturing love is needed to understand the child's fear and pain and not belittle or devalue the child.

Second, plan your *Goals.* Since you assessed that faith is low, then your first goal is to build faith. Help your child discover God's character, that he didn't promise his children that they would never experience pain, but he did promise to be with them even in the arena with the lions (or dogs). God promised to bring good out of every pain (Rom. 8:28). Help your child discover God's good plan in the midst of the problem. Pray with your child, asking God to bring good, for his glory, from the difficulty. Read Bible stories about children facing danger but seeing God at work.

Help children visualize themselves drawing the sword of the Spirit (i.e., Bible verses they have memorized like "I will trust and not be afraid" [Isa. 12:2]) and whacking the fiery darts of fear with which the enemy tries to cripple them. Bible memory can be helpful. (See Table 5–1, page 67, for some Scriptures that may help.)

Second, plan what work you can do to build faith. Model brave behavior and let your child see you playing, unharmed, with gentle dogs. Apply "systematic desensitization" and model not being afraid. How? An adult slowly approaches the feared object and shows the child that nothing bad happens. Then the adult invites the child to make a small approach. For example, children who are phobic over puppies may be invited first to look at pictures of people enjoying playing with puppies. The adult may ask the child to imagine himself or herself getting close to and eventually petting a gentle puppy. At another time, the adult may hold and pet a puppy as the child watches. After many times watching, breathing slowly, and learning to calm himself or herself, the child may be invited to touch the puppy's back, while an adult holds the puppy. Later, the child can stroke the puppy's back, then head, hold the puppy, and finally play with it. Small steps over many weeks or months help. After a child can play with one gentle dog or puppy, others can be introduced until the fears are controlled.

Children can also be taught how to relabel fearful sensations (pounding heart, cold feet) as "excitement" instead of "fear" when faced with a scary but nonharmful situation. This too takes time and work.

Third, plan to practice love. How can you value your child more? Don't belittle the child's fear or make fun of the fear. Humor rarely works to alleviate extreme fears—it makes the child feel misunderstood and devalued. Also, for phobias, do not use the sink-or-swim method, forcing the child to face the danger head on. That would be like asking someone with a leg cast to run a marathon. The child needs healing first.

In the goal-planning stage of AGAPE, ask God to show you how to better disciple your child through this ordeal. Your child will feel valued as you try to understand the fears and spend time helping your child overcome his or her fears. You might combine desensitization training with teaching your fearful child about God's protection and providence.

Take the *Actions* you have planned, which will take many days. Remember to seek God's help. Don't attempt to solve any problem without the Lord's strength and guidance.

Remember to *Persevere*. Keep working systematically and lovingly. It takes effort to cast all of one's anxieties on Jesus (1 Pet. 5:7), instead of continuing to carry them.

Evaluate your progress in helping your child conquer the problem. Evaluate whether faith has been strengthened in a loving way.

Activity: To build a foundation of faith, list (with your spouse if appropriate) some trust-building family activities that fit your time, finances, and interests (i.e., backpacking, rock-climbing, hiking, boating, writing stories together, creating a group art project, traveling, playing board games, visiting historical sites or museums together). Let your children choose from among your ideas. Put those plans on your calendar. Do them. Keeping your word builds trust.

Disobedience and Rebellion

Problems majoring in faith. Disobedience and rebellion major in weaknesses in faith. Rebellion is willfully resisting authority, which undermines trust in God, who is the supreme authority. While parents are certainly not perfect authorities, parents are one of God's most important ways of teaching humans to trust. But what do parents do when their children refuse to trust them? Is that always rebellion?

Developing autonomy. "I can do it," yells a frustrated two-year-old Barbara. Her shoe laces are hopelessly tangled, but she is determined that she can tie her own shoes. Is that rebellion? No. Barbara is developing a sense of identity or autonomy. She must separate from her parents, or she will not develop a healthy personality in which she can gain faith, discover the work God has created her to do, and learn to love God and others (faith working through love).

However, if her parent is late to an appointment, the parent (by not planning enough time for Barbara to dress herself) may inadvertently push Barbara into a deliberate refusal, which is rebellion. When Barbara continues to assert her independence even after her parent says that it is time to go, then Barbara's sense of autonomy and control become out of balance, nontrusting, and (therefore) rebellious. Instead of helping her mature in faith, rebellion can lead to a distorted self-importance, if the rebellion is not corrected.

Parents need to teach children skills so that they can succeed and thus develop a sense of who they are, and parents need to set up the environment so that children can successfully experiment, explore, and discover. However, parents also need to give children balance. For the strong, determined child who never wants help, even when he or she is crying from frustration, parents need to offer help, patiently breaking down the process into simple steps, and demonstrating each step, letting the child follow the steps. Ask, "May I show you how to get started? Then you can do it. Here's the first part. Can you do this? Good! You are so grown up! Here's what you do next . . ." For the child who wants parents to do it all, parents need to encourage that child to try. Say, "You can do it! This is step one. Try step one. No, I won't do it for you, but I'll help you learn how to do it." Through such teaching the parent values the child, helps him or her feel capable, and balances independence and teachability.

Some examples of rebellion are as follows. If you gave the child a warning, "When the buzzer goes off, it will be time to go," and you are sure the child heard you, and the child refuses to mind, that's rebellion. If the child knowingly speaks disrespectfully to you or others, argues with you after having expressed an opinion and being told why a decision was made, and challenges authority in head-on confrontation, that's rebellion. Children are commanded in Scripture to obey and honor their parents (Deut. 5:16; Matt. 19:19; Mark 7:10; Eph. 6:2; Col. 3:20).

But this does not come naturally. Parents must teach children to honor, obey, and trust, so that one day they will honor, obey, and trust their heavenly Father (Deut. 4:9–10; 6:7). If children learn that they can disobey authority without negative consequences, their faith and trust are severely damaged. Parents build this trust by patient teaching, with consistent praise for good attitudes and behaviors, and punishment for bad.

Instant AGAPE. Encourage autonomy, but set limits so that you can encourage trust. Punish rebellion. However, it is not always easy to tell which behaviors to punish. When in doubt, apply Instant AGAPE. For example, a friend was trying to get some work done while her two-year-old and four-year-old boys watched *Mr. Rogers.* Paul, the older child, decided to help Mama fix lunch. He knew that he was not allowed to touch the stove. So he took some eggs, a bowl of fruit cocktail, and some bacon out of the refrigerator. But how to heat them? Inspiration struck. *The clothes dryer made things hot,* he thought. *Boy, won't Mama be happy I helped her with lunch?*

When Paul showed Sharon the complete meal he had "fixed" in the dryer, she almost lost it. But she silently prayed, gulped, and praised Paul's desire to help. She explained that the dryer was for clothes, not food, but praised his motives. (Silently she thanked the Lord that Paul was too short to turn on the dryer.)

In cases like this, as in many child-parent problems, parents must apply AGAPE quickly. The more you use it, the more automatic it will become. Sharon quickly and prayerfully *assessed* that the problem was not rebellion or any behavior requiring punishment, other than helping clean up the mess. She already had the *goals* of valuing and building up her children, and of training them in godliness, so she reminded herself of those goals as she was tempted to get angry at the mess. She took *action* by praising her son for trying to be helpful (she valued him), and she also taught him what the dryer was for. Sharon *persevered* by taking time to teach Paul what to do next time, not only in words but by letting him help her fix lunch correctly. As she *evaluated* her actions, she was pleased to see that her son had (she hoped) learned not to put food in the dryer. He had learned that he was a helpful boy who was growing in godliness, and that his mother (and God) appreciated his efforts.

Rejection of Parental Values

Steve's story. Gary and Melissa love each other, their children, and the Lord. A few years ago they found out that their son, Steve, was addicted to drugs. Steve was also sexually active and seemed to have rejected everything his parents stood for. Gary and Melissa's hearts felt like they would explode. At first, they didn't want to tell anyone. They felt as if they had failed as parents, and the pain was nearly unbearable. They took Steve to a Christian drug treatment program where he slowly recovered.

During Steve's treatment, they too learned. Gary discovered that being a workaholic was a form of addiction. Workaholism is more socially acceptable in our culture than are alcoholism and drug addictions, but workaholism can devastate a family who desperately needs the time, love, and attention of their dad. Gary began giving more time to his family.

Gary and Melissa also discovered that they had wanted control so much that they had not let Steve make enough decisions. They had set curfews that Steve thought were unfair. Instead of talking over his feelings, Steve had rebelled, and the more he had rebelled, the more his parents had tried to control him. They felt they couldn't give him more freedom until he showed more responsibility. The power struggle had escalated until the only communication was fighting and yelling. After Steve's treatment, Gary and Melissa let Steve have more control in setting rules that affected him. Gary and Melissa didn't take responsibility for Steve's behavior. However, they understood that they could change their own behavior to help.

Why do some teens reject parental values? There are many reasons why children reject their parents' values. The rejection of the parents' values appears to be highly connected with whether the parents "walk their talk." Anolik (1983), Berger (1988), Rice and Grusec (1975), and Rushton (1975) found that children were more likely to adhere to their parents' morals if their parents both taught high morals and lived by the same standards than if parents only taught them. Of course, teaching is better than no teaching, but teaching plus living is most effective. An excellent book is *Teaching Children Values* by Linda and Richard Eyre (1993).

Probably the greatest heartbreaker for Christian parents is when a child rejects their values. Rejection of Christian values can mean rejecting Christ himself, with eternal consequences. As important as it is, though, as a parent *you must not turn faith into a power struggle*, which will not achieve the ends you desire. It will push your teen further from you and from Jesus.

Dealing with a teen's crisis in faith. How can you promote faith in your teen without making it a control issue?

- *Before* the teen years, help your children experience the reality of Christ. Pray with them about their needs, so they can see God work.
- Help them enjoy church.
- Discuss moral issues openly as a family, encouraging your children to think and talk.
- Encourage your teen to ask questions. Be available to answer questions without giving the message, "How can you ask that?" If your teen likes to read, have good books on hand to help him or her find answers.

- Show your teen that you care. A teen is not too old for hugs, pats on the back, smiles, and "Hey world" shouts. Listen to your teen. Accept your teen's feelings as real and valid.
- Pray for his or her concerns.
- Confess to your children your sins that affect them and ask their forgiveness. Ask them to pray for you about those qualities in you that are hurting or angering them.
- Let your teen see godly adults having healthy fun.
- Help your teen find godly friends who accept and love him or her.

What if an adolescent openly rejects Christ? How should you respond?

- Don't preach.
- Pray. Ask God to fill your teen's room, workplace, car, dorm room, and anywhere else he or she will be, with his Holy Spirit to woo the teen back to him. God loves your teen more than you do.
- Ask what turned the teen away. Listen intently. Don't get defensive, argue, or justify. If you did something wrong, ask forgiveness. Ask the teen to help you change, if there is something you should change. If he or she reveals an unmet need, ask how you can help meet it.
- Ask God to show you his view of your own lifestyle to see if it might be changed to help your child. Do you do things that devalue God in your teen's eyes? Ask God. He'll show you. But be willing to change with God's help.

Unmet needs. The problems between Steve and his parents began, in part, because neither Steve nor his parents felt their needs were being met. Both needed intimacy and neither felt valued or respected by the other. Both needed distance at times and felt a loss of control. As Steve tried to pull away, the parents felt their grasp slipping, so they clamped down. Steve and his parents became enmeshed in a power struggle. Steve was trying to find a sense of identity—of who he was apart from his parents. As he pulled away, though, his parents lost something of their identity—as parents. As the struggle escalated, both parents and Steve concentrated more on which of their *own* needs were being frustrated. They reacted by increasing their attempts to meet their own needs through power.

To stop such struggles, parents must decide to set aside their own needs for a while in an attempt to meet their teens' (and ultimately their own) needs more fully. If parents impose a solution by coercion, the results often backfire. The best solutions come when the parents love enough to listen and understand and meet their teens' needs before their own.

Question: In your home, are your teen's and your own needs being met? If not, someone has to change. Let it be you.

Activity: Do you know what your teen needs? Examine Table 5–2. Are those needs being met? Would your teen agree with your evaluation?

Table 5–2
Adolescents' Needs

Intimacy:	Teens need to feel that they belong, both in their family and with peers. Let them know you want them around. Help them develop social skills. Give opportunities for team activities, youth groups, etc. Let them invite friends over. Encourage teens to express their needs and feelings in kind, respectful ways.
Distance:	Teens need time alone to think and sort through ideas and feelings that they never had in childhood. Too much alone time

could mean avoiding a challenge (fear of failure), depression, drugs, or other problems. So be aware if they become snappy, overly moody, or seem very sad. Apply AGAPE and get help. Ask if your teen needs to talk (if so, you listen), or needs time alone.

Control or Power: Teens need to be allowed to make more decisions than they made as children, and to be consulted in family decisions. That values them and builds their confidence.

Identity: Adolescents need to become separate adults. They need to discover who they are, why they were created, with what gifts, and for what purpose. Encourage them. Tell them what good you see in them.

Achievement: Teens have a need to achieve, to meet a challenge and conquer it. Provide healthy opportunities within their capabilities and interests to meet this need.

Practicing Faith Working through Love with Teens

Let's again apply AGAPE. If you are having trouble with adolescent rebellion, *Assess* the problem carefully. The problem is not really the fighting and disobedience. Those are symptoms. The underlying problem is that neither the parents' nor the teen's needs are being met, and both are trying to meet their own needs in unhealthy ways. Examine your adolescent's needs and ask yourself how you can meet those needs in a way that won't lead to conflict. Look through the glasses of faith working through love. Jesus commanded people to love and encourage. If you have not been showing as much valuing love as your adolescent needs, show more.

Goal planning is next. It is not easy to show valuing love if your teen has fallen into a negative, obnoxious pattern to get attention. Ask God to show you what to praise. Goal planning must include discovering new ways to meet your teen's needs. Look again at Table 5–2. What needs can you meet?

Take the *Actions* you've planned and *Persevere*. By applying faith working through love, you can help make your teen's wings strong, so he or she can fly. Strong wings that are caged beat the bars for release. Weak wings that fly prematurely struggle to stay airborne. If your teen is determined to fly with underdeveloped wings, then together create opportunities for flight in safe settings to train strength into those wings.

Evaluate your progress. If progress is slow, again check Table 5–2 for other needs that may not be met. Praise even small steps in the desired direction.

Weaknesses in Work

School Problems and Trouble Making

School problems and making trouble are often *caused* by weaknesses in valuing love, but *show up* as failures in work. School problems sometimes characterize children who have been belittled for their efforts and are afraid to try at schoolwork. Unconsciously they may feel that if they don't try, then they can blame their failure on lack of effort instead of on lack of intelligence, which they fear. Trouble making problems often characterize children who are more sensitive than they seem. Both school problems and trouble making are often cries for attention or for peer acceptance (i.e., valuing love). The child responds by failure to work. Many underachievers are hurting deeply from low self-esteem, but are outwardly saying, "I don't care if I do badly." They may act up, drop out, or become class clowns instead of admitting that they cannot read or understand the work. An undiscovered learning disability may be an underlying cause. (Ask your local school to test your child if you suspect a learning disability.)

The need to be loved by family and peers is so important that many older children will do even destructive things to belong. Jason committed a robbery with some friends. He was so hungry for affection and for someone to care enough to set limits that he did whatever the "friends" said. He had no hobbies. No one had taught him sports or skills to start friendships. He seldom received praise for his prosocial efforts. Criticism was frequent. He never felt he belonged. A delinquent peer group accepted him—if he would do what they did.

If your child is making trouble at school it is time to intervene. Don't wait and hope things will get better. Apply AGAPE.

Assess the problem. Try to find out what is behind the trouble making. The child probably won't know why he or she is doing destructive things. Try to discern the unmet needs. (See page 53 and Table 5–2, page 79.)

Set *Goals*, then take *Action*. Whatever your child's age, if the child's poor work is a cry for attention, spend time and help him or her build skills. Praise small successes until the child gains enough confidence to try again and succeed. Keep praising effort. Give attention for on-task, nondisruptive behaviors. Let your son or daughter try new skills in the summer to see what sparks his or her interest. Sports, dancing, art, music, drama, chess, computers, camping, nature studies, and creative writing can build self-esteem and help a child want to *work* toward a goal.

Persevere until you find what works for your child. One shy twelve-year-old boy was not working at his potential in school and his mother was concerned about him. She introduced him to many sports and activities, but none clicked. Then she suggested ballroom dancing. For him, that was the turn around. He loved it, took lessons, found a sweet partner, practiced hard, and began competing. His grades shot up and his confidence soared. He is still shy, but he no longer acts up to get attention.

Teaching your child doesn't have to be expensive. Teach the skills yourself whenever you can and seek low-cost or sliding-scale lessons for activities. When Christen was interested in gymnastics, we couldn't afford the lessons. The gymnastics coach at a local high school helped us contact a student on the team who gave Christen a few inexpensive lessons. Once Christen made the school team, lessons were free. Barter. "I'll baby-sit your children or upholster your couch if you'll teach my child tennis the same number of hours." God will show you creative ways to meet your children's needs if you will ask him and search for his provision.

Evaluation isn't always easy. Success may show up in various forms, such as better grades, new friends, enjoying sports, drama, or clubs, or improved communication between you and your child. Even after improvement occurs, keep encouraging the good, and don't allow yourself to fall back into critical, negative patterns, or your child's failures may return.

Question: Do you usually praise only high achievement? If so, force yourself to praise any effort in the right direction. Praise even the beginning efforts of an underachiever. Keep praising regardless of the child's response. Eventually, praise will sink in and heal.

Question: Look at your child objectively. Ask God to show you areas of lack and of giftedness. What can you do to help build skills and encourage gifts? Write specific plans.

Applying Faith Working through Love

We often pray over our children after they are asleep. If your child is struggling with school, pray (*not* in his or her hearing or he or she may take it as criticism) for God to give your child a desire to learn and for God to give you insights into what is behind the school problems. Have faith that God longs to give you wisdom, guide you, and help your child. Have faith in your child and find ways to show that you believe in him or her.

"If you love someone . . . you will always believe in him (even when he has disappointed you repeatedly), always expect the best of him, and always stand your ground in defending him" (1 Cor. 13:7 LB). Encourage, teach skills patiently, set attainable goals together, then expect small positive steps and rejoice in the progress.

The week after writing the first draft of this chapter, we had an opportunity to retest the AGAPE technique for solving family problems. Our family took a one-week camping vacation in Tennessee's Great Smokey Mountain National Park. With six people in a van, organization is important. The first two days the children did not put things away correctly. The van was a disaster area and I (Kirby) was frustrated at not being able to find needed items. In desperation, Ev and I applied AGAPE.

First we *Assessed.* Perhaps the children didn't know exactly where things belonged. (I doubted that at first. Although I was sure the disorderliness was a conspiracy to destroy my sanity, I had to admit to the possibility that the children didn't know where things belonged.) I also realized that the lack of order bothered me because I felt like a failure as a mother because I had not yet fully trained our children to be orderly. As I got upset, I brought out fussing and arguing in the children, which made us all angry and less likely to cooperate. Instead of valuing and appreciating what the children did, I judged them. So I decided to center on where *I* could change. I'd naturally rather have blamed the children, but that wouldn't have solved anything, and I wanted a cure.

We then planned our *Goals* and took the following *Actions.* We made sure that everyone understood where each item belonged. I then stayed away from the car and let the children find the needed items. That way I didn't get angry at seeing any mess, and I could thank and praise them for their help. Of course, as they tried to find items, they became aware of the natural consequences of not putting things away properly and they soon began to store items in their proper containers. I prayed often for a loving, patient attitude. I also spoke with each child who had argued with me, and together we decided to try harder to show valuing love and respect to one another.

I *Persevered.* I was tempted several times to go into the car and fuss again, but each time I stopped (often with Ev's gentle reminder), asked for help, and thanked the child instead. My changed attitude affected the atmosphere of the entire family.

In *Evaluation*, I'm continually amazed at how quickly our emotions can change. The first two days of our trip I was ready to never take the children camping again until they learned order, which would have solved nothing. The remainder of the trip we had a great time, laughing, not complaining, hiking, and loving being together.

Weaknesses in Love

Sibling Rivalry and Family Fighting

Sibling rivalry. Fred called out, "Ann, Mama's home with your new brother!"

Five-year-old Ann looked warily at the wrinkled bundle and asked, "Can I play with him?"

"No, he's too little."

"But you said he'd be a playmate."

Later as Rose nursed baby brother, Ann wanted Rose to read to her. "Not now, Ann. I'm feeding Seth."

That night Ann wet her bed. Two months later, she hit Seth. She repeatedly said she hated him.

This is sibling rivalry. Sibling rivalry can be defined as competition with a sibling due to a child's insecurity from feeling less valuable than the sibling. Sibling rivalry is a problem in valuing love.

The solutions major in work, as well as valuing love. Generally, your work will involve planning and carrying out ways to build the self-esteem of the older child as you involve him or her in helping the younger. See Table 5–3 for some steps you can take to minimize sibling rivalry.

Table 5–3
Minimizing Sibling Rivalry

Expectations:	Do not expect fighting. Children usually try to live up to their parents' expectations. Let them know that you expect them to love each other. Then model and teach valuing love.
Preparation:	Prepare an older child for a new baby's arrival ahead of time with *realistic* expectations.
Participation:	Let the older child participate in the care of the infant in as many ways as his or her maturity will safely allow (wash the baby's feet, show the baby pictures, talk to the baby). This "work" helps the older child feel valued and builds love.
Attention:	Spend time cuddling and reading with your older children, even while nursing the baby. Also spend time with each of them alone, no matter how busy you are. Be sure that you continue to value each older child with attention for his or her good behavior. Tell each child how much you appreciate his or her help. Otherwise, misbehavior may begin to attract your attention, and a negative cycle will start.
Avoid Regression:	If an older child was toilet trained and now has accidents, or returns to thumb sucking, etc., this shows a need for attention, due to insecurity. Give as little attention as possible to the regressive behaviors, but immediately

give more positive attention for grown-up activities. Encourage, compliment, build up your child, spend time with him or her doing grown-up things, like cooking or reading together, and he or she *will* act more grown up.

Model and Teach: Social skills are not inborn. Teach children how to show love in healthy ways

Don't Compare: Sibling rivalry can show up as unhealthy comparisons or too much competition. It can show up as a fear of failure that keeps a child from competing at all. You can help by valuing and accepting each child. Point out and rejoice in each child's gifts. Give each child opportunities to enhance his or her gifts.

Don't compare siblings. For example, one of our friends has two girls close in age. The older is artistic and creative. The younger girl loves math and spelling and is moving rapidly in academic areas. The older was showing signs of insecurity, which was coming out as fierce competition.

One night the father explained to the older daughter that God gives each of his children different gifts, each equally valuable to God. Her father asked her what she thought some of her gifts were, and added ones he saw in her. They also discussed her younger sister's gifts.

A few days later the older girl told her mother about a class spelling bee. Just as the mother was about to ask her how she had done, she said, "Remember, Mama, one of my gifts from God is art, not spelling." The child knew she no longer had to compete and fall short. She too had special gifts from her heavenly Father that her parents valued. (Of course, the mother still insisted the girl study spelling.)

Question: Ask God to show you if you are valuing each child equally. Our society values beauty, brains, and brawn.

It is easy for such biases to creep into our thinking. Are you following what society or Christ values? Do you love each child regardless of his or her giftedness? Are you enjoying each child individually, or spending more time with one?

Activity: Write each of your children's names. Under each, write ten personality or character qualities you appreciate about that child. This is not a list of their achievements. This is a chance for you to see what qualities you value in each child, so you can tell each one.

Family fighting. Josie stormed into her sister's room, "Who told you that you could use my new shirt?"

Casey whined, "You aren't using it."

"Maybe I was planning on wearing it later today. Did you ever think about that?"

Casey threw the blouse at her sister and shouted, "Just take it. I didn't want the ugly rag any way."

"Fine—I'm never talking to you again." Josie stormed out, slamming the door. Casey threw a stuffed animal at the door and screamed.

If these were your children, how could you apply AGAPE? First, *Assess* what is causing the fighting. Family fighting is due to a weakness in love and in work. *If I get my way, I must be valuable,* people think. Then they do hurtful actions to get their way. Such problems are solved by work that builds valuing love. Since love is a choice of actions, from which feelings follow, then the choice to work or act in a way that values another person makes fertile ground in which loving feelings can grow.

Here are some ways to stop family fighting. Use these in your *Goal planning* and *Action. Persevere* and *Evaluate* the effects of each way you use.

1. Eliminate the situations or set limits in areas that have brought out fighting in the past.

- If the problem is not honoring another person's property, model and teach your children to show respect by asking, "Do you need your green earrings today, or may I use them?" That puts the other's needs and desires before your own.

- If fights occur because one child teases another, teach the screecher to communicate differently and teach the teaser better ways to get attention or show affection. Preschoolers and elementary-aged children often enjoy role-playing good ways to work out differences. Some teens will respond to this, if you let them come up with the answers.

- Most fights between teens and parents are over curfews, money, and chores (Montemayor 1983). Let your preteen or teen help you set fair rules for each of those areas and any other potentially explosive areas. Decide *together* acceptable limits, during nonfighting times, then give the teen freedom within those limits.

2. During non-angry times, encourage your children to help one another. We made a yarn doll with a sign on it that reads, "I did this because I love you." If a child does a chore for a sibling, the child puts the doll in that spot. (See also Appendix A for the "Building Godly Character Game.")

3. Recognize if the fight is a power struggle. In power struggles the real issue is who gets to make the rules. Set up a family discussion to empower everyone by gathering opinions, taking votes, and listening to each person's input.

4. Physically stop bad fights. Send the fighters to different rooms and give them "work" that teaches them to value and respect their sibling. The "work" may be to write or draw their feelings, or whatever helps them to calm down. Once they are calm enough to want to find solutions, have them consider what their part was in the fight and determine what they can do to change their own behavior. Another tech-

nique that sometimes is helpful is to ask both fighters to write ten qualities about their sibling that they like.

5. Teach later, not in the heat of the moment. If children are very angry, or if they are middle schoolers or older, they may resist your intervention. Adolescents need to begin working out their own problems using the skills you have modeled and taught them when they were younger. If they have not been taught how to communicate with valuing love (even when they are angry), how to listen to understand the other's point of view, and how to admit when they are wrong, then teach them. But not in the heat of conflict. When you are alone with one child, listen to his or her feelings. Ask the older child to help you build up the younger sibling. Explain that the younger one may be acting obnoxiously because he or she wants the older one's attention. Ask the older sibling to invite the younger to do something they both enjoy. For teenagers, who are old enough to see from the other's viewpoint, help each one understand the other and encourage both to think of creative ways to build love. Then praise their efforts. See Table 5–4 for some verses that show God's plan for family peace.

Table 5–4
Scripture on God's Plan for Family Peace

Isaiah 32:18	"My people will live in peaceful dwelling places, in secure homes, in undisturbed places of rest" (NIV).
Ephesians 4:26, 27	"Do not let the sun go down while you are still angry, and do not give the devil a foothold" (NIV).
Proverbs 15:1	"A gentle answer turns away wrath, but *a harsh word stirs up anger*" (NIV).
Proverbs 15:4	"A (gentle, RSV) tongue that brings healing is a tree of life" (NIV).
Proverbs 17:1	"Better a dry crust with peace and quiet than a house full of feasting, with strife" (NIV).

Proverbs 17:9	"Love forgets mistakes, nagging about them parts the best of friends" (LB).
Proverbs 19:18	"Discipline your son, while there is hope, but *do not indulge your angry resentments* by undue chastisements and set yourself to his ruin" (AB).
Proverbs 21:9	"Better to live on a corner of the roof than share a house with a quarrelsome wife" (or any family member) (NIV).
1 Cor. 13:5b	"(Love) keeps no record of wrongs" (NIV).
Colossians 3:13	"Bear with each other and forgive whatever grievances you may have against one another. Forgive as the LORD forgave you" (NIV).
Psalms 101:2, 3b	"I will be careful to lead a blameless life. . . . I will walk in my house with blameless heart. I will set before my eyes no vile thing" (NIV).
James 3:16	"For wherever there is jealousy (envy) and contention (rivalry and selfish ambition) there will also be confusion (unrest, disharmony, rebellion) and all sorts of evil and vile practices" (AB).

Whining

"It's mine! But I want it! Maaamaaa!"

Whining is talking in a tone that disturbs the very nerve fibers of an already worn out, but previously sane, adult. Children notice a whiny voice in another child, but they must be taught to recognize it in themselves. Whining is shrill and pouting. The whine says, "You're treating me unfairly. Don't you know who I am? I am the center of my universe. I deserve better treatment. I want my way."

Whining is a problem in valuing love. It values the self above anyone else. Young children are egocentric (centered on self) in their natural brain development. Their brain must mature through age and experience before they can be taught that some of their actions are selfish. Parents must *train* young children to think of others, using rewards and punishment. When they are older, children develop understanding.

Temper Tantrums

Tantrums, like whining, are a problem in valuing. Tantrums are whining run amok. Tantrums say, "I want my way, and I want it *now* or you'll be sorry you didn't treat me right." Tantrums involve shrill yelling or screaming. Sometimes children will throw themselves onto the floor, kicking and pounding the floor while screaming. Some will hit themselves or beat their heads. Throwing a tantrum is violent intimidation. Tantrums take advantage of parents who feel they are too tired to deal with the screaming or too embarrassed because the tantrum occurs in front of friends or in a public place. The success of a tantrum depends on the parents' *in*consistency.

Before parents can apply AGAPE to whining or tantrums, they must be convinced that change is possible. Children can unlearn tantrums.

Scotty was age two. Whenever Scotty didn't get his way he threw a tantrum. His mother thought that he couldn't help the tantrums. One day, Scotty didn't get his way and was gearing up for a tantrum, when he looked at the floor. It was hard. So Scotty went into a room with a rug and threw his tantrum there. He knew exactly what he was doing.

Nora, a hyperactive child, threw uncontrollable tantrums until one day she threw one on a terrazzo (cement-like) floor. It hurt. She never threw another. Tantrums can be unlearned.

As parents *Assess* the situation, by looking through the glasses of faith working through love, they see that the child has a weakness in love. The child wants his or her way, regardless of what others need. The child is not valuing others. The child may also want to feel more valued by the parent. Parents must consider how they can show more valuing love to their child and how they can train their child to value others.

Goal planning for whining and tantrums involves applying a four-step process: (1) stop giving attention for bad behavior and *never* give children what they want when they are tantruming or whining; (2) give positive attention (praise, hugs) for good behavior; (3) when possible, avoid situations that bring on the misbehaviors; and (4) teach the child that he or she must value (love) others besides himself or herself. (See Table 5–5 for a quick summary of how to carry out these four steps.) Plan how to implement these steps with your child.

Table 5–5
A Four-Step Method for Dealing with Failures in Love

Step 1: Stop giving attention for bad behavior.

- Make sure that the child understands exactly which behavior to stop.
- Briefly tell the child that you will ignore the bad behavior. Say, "I won't pay attention to you while you're throwing a tantrum. I'll be back when you're ready to talk and play."
- Expect an "extinction burst." When you first ignore a bad behavior, a child will get worse before getting better. He or she may test to see if you will keep ignoring the bad behavior or if you will lose your temper if the child gets louder. Stand your ground.

Step 2: Give positive attention for good behavior.

- Tell the child, in terms he or she can understand, what specific behavior you expect in place of the bad behavior.
- Immediately notice and give good attention (praise, cheer, clap, hug) for the desired behavior.
- Praise *consistently* and *specifically*. A child will do what gets attention.

Step 3. When possible, avoid situations that you've learned bring on such misbehaviors.

- Set up the environment to make positive encounters more likely by giving early warnings, making consequences clear, and giving choices within acceptable limits.
- Anticipate and meet your child's needs. For example, if your child is usually grumpy two hours after a meal, then anticipate

and give a small, healthy snack *before* he or she gets grumpy. If your child is hard to control when he or she gets overtired, put the child down for a rest *before* he or she goes into overdrive. Don't pack too much into a day.

- Avoid inconsistency. Routines help children.
- If you have been unable to avoid the misbehavior in a public place, don't be intimidated into inaction. Leave the public place as soon as possible and discipline the child in private.

Step 4: Teach the child to value (love) others besides himself or herself.

- Tailor your teaching to the age of the child.
- When the child is rested and happy, before any more incidents of whining, tantrums, or aggression occur, play games and do activities that train your child to think about others. When you watch a show or read together, ask the child, "How do you think that would feel? Do you think that child is sad?" Help your child learn to recognize facial expressions that show another's need. Practice sharing, hugging, making friends, and other desired behaviors by simple role plays and practice games. Praise good attempts. (See Appendix A, the Building Godly Character Game.)

Take *Action* by working through each step. With tantrums and whining, *Perseverance* is essential. Tantrums depend upon parents' inconsistency of spanking one time, ignoring the next, scolding the next, understanding another time, screaming, then ignoring again.

Evaluation for whining and tantrums is straightforward. They either stop or continue. If tantrums have stopped but then start again, the child is testing to see if you will give in. Don't.

Aggression

Aggression is primarily a weakness in love. The aggressive child values his or her own needs above others and imposes his or her will on others by force. The child may hit, bully, or intimidate peers and even parents. He or she may threaten, yell, or demand. The use of force devalues others.

One technique, by itself, will not work for every aggressive child. Motivations and causes may be different. In all cases, though, train the child in what is expected and praise good behaviors immediately. Withhold attention for bad behavior, but never withhold love.

Larry Christenson, author of *The Christian Family* (1970) and an excellent tape series of the same title, told two true stories. In one, a spanking was given to a child who had never before been held accountable for his actions. It turned his life around. In the other, a young juvenile delinquent, who had been punished all of his life, was sent to a Christian camp, run by Christenson's father. One night, the boys got out of control. The pastor entered the room and said, "Maybe some of you didn't understand, but we need it quiet here so we can plan some activities for you. Apparently I need someone to sort of take charge in here." The pastor pointed to the particularly defiant boy and said, "Why don't you just take charge for me in here?"

"Me? Leave it to me," he said.

There was no more noise that night. Giving value and undeserved trust to that teen transformed his life. He still had some rough times, but he later accepted Jesus and had a ministry with prisoners.

One life was made better because someone loved a child enough to punish wrong behavior. Another life was changed because someone expected good and dared to trust a teen who didn't deserve it. No one method will stop aggression in all children. It is helpful to understand the *causes* for the aggressive behavior.

Assess what is behind your child's aggressive behavior. Childhood aggression has been shown to be affected by at least five factors: (a) viewing television and movie violence (Liebert and Sprafkin 1988), (b) inability to see oneself and one's actions from another's perspective (Chalmers and Townsend 1990; Feshbach and Feshbach 1982), (c) poor academic or physical performance (causing low self-esteem which comes out as aggression in some children), (d) seeing aggression modeled at home (Emery 1989; Holden and

Ritchie 1991), and (c) feeling anger at a situation that one feels powerless to change (death, divorce, father absence, a learning disability, loss of a friend, a handicap, etc.) (Hetherington and Camara 1984; Johnson 1993).

Set *Goals* for *Action*. To help the child reduce aggression and to build a more loving spirit, the parent should deal with whichever of the above factors are present and should provide a context of faith and love for the child to work on reducing the aggression. Different causes need a different action plan.

Reduce viewing of television and movie violence. If a child copies violence he or she has observed in movies or on television, explain that you feel partly responsible for having let the child watch movies that taught him or her to hurt people. As a family, you might decide not to have violent movies or TV shows in your home, which may be a sacrifice for those who like action-adventure movies. Or, you may tell the aggressive child, "Daddy can watch action movies because he doesn't copy the violence he sees. When you learn to act kindly and not hurt other people, then we will know you are old enough to watch movies or television without copying the bad behavior." Children under age eight may even copy violence seen in cartoons (Collins et al. 1978).

You may want to memorize what some Scriptures say about what we choose to watch or think about. Psalm 101:2, 3 says, "I will give heed to the way that is blameless. . . . I will not set before my eyes anything that is base." Philippians 4:8 says, "Whatsoever is true . . . honorable . . . just . . . pure . . . lovely . . . gracious. . . , think upon these."

Build empathy. If the child has trouble seeing things from the viewpoint of the one he or she hurt, role play with the child. You play the aggressor and do to your child what he or she has done to other children (excluding physical damage). Then discuss how such actions make your child feel. Also show your child alternative, nonaggressive ways to communicate.

Help defeat inferiority. If a child feels inferior and uses force to build up himself or herself, then help the child (a) feel valued and loved and (b) be more successful at difficult tasks. If academics are troublesome, help the child learn to study or perhaps get tutoring in the weak areas. If inferiority feelings stem from poor physical ability, enhance physical skills through involving the child in physical activities. Teach skills patiently. Make learning fun. Praise positive effort.

Don't model aggression at home. Do you lose your temper or act aggressively? If so, then ask the Lord to help you change to more loving methods of interacting with your family. If a member of your family is abusive, get help immediately. Abuse breeds more abuse.

Help deal with anger productively. Anger is a common response to feeling out of control. Help your children recognize when they feel out of control. Help them learn what to say to themselves to avoid angry outbursts. For example, "I lost that game, but I'm learning to play better. Jesus, please help me be kind to my opponent."

Help your children know that God is in control. God can even bring good out of painful situations. Seeing this not only provides a sense of control for children but also builds them into stronger disciples of Christ. Also help children gain skills in areas that they *can* control. When your children are angry or frustrated, show that you understand, but also help them learn better ways to handle anger and frustration, such as drawing or writing about their feelings. Praise positive efforts.

Deal with instances of aggression. Besides building an attitude of faith working through love to replace the aggressive attitude, deal firmly with aggressive behaviors. Find out what is behind an act of aggression. Ask, "Why did you punch Jimmy?" Then *listen* to the answer. Your child may say, "He took my ball." Show that you understand how your child felt, perhaps saying, "I'll bet that made you feel angry. I know how that feels." State the rule. Say, "Hitting hurts people. I can't allow you to hurt anyone. When you are angry, you should talk. Don't hit."

Consider whether you are dealing with a first or repeated offense, and take action. If the child is young and this is a first offense, a short timeout in which he or she gets no attention until he or she is ready to apologize may be enough to end such misbehavior, especially if the child soon receives praise for gentle, kind behavior. If this is a repeat offense, then it is time to *Persevere*. You may need to do to your child a gentler version of what he or she did to the other child, saying, "You hurt Mary when you pulled her hair. You need to know how much it hurts so that you won't do that again. I'm going to pull your hair so that you know how it feels." (Your goal is to teach empathy, not to inflict harm on your child.) Then say, "Do you see how that hurts when someone pulls your hair? Are you going to pull hair again?" Let the child apologize to the one he or she has hurt. Praise cooperative behavior as soon as possible. Say, "I'm glad you are sharing your toys. How grown up and kind you are becoming!"

If children use aggression to gain your attention, ignore aggressive behaviors, unless you must rescue a hurt child. At the same time, give lots of attention for kind behavior. Children learn to do more of what gets attention and less of what is ignored.

With older children, use role playing to train new behaviors to replace aggressive behaviors. Remember to *Persevere* with praise for the good as well as with punishment or ignoring for the bad.

Your *Evaluation* should tell you more than just if the aggressive behavior has stopped. Is your child also feeling better about himself or herself? You want children to repent of wrong actions, not feel worthless. Recognizing feelings, understanding why children made the choices they did, and helping them see that there are kind ways to handle those feelings, values children as you train them.

Closing

Throughout this book we've sketched a blueprint of parenting that we believe is consistent with God's word, one that is based on faith, work, and valuing love. If you can get the blueprint into your spirit, you won't necessarily deal flawlessly with every problem your child has or prevent all pain. Nor will you be completely free of feelings that you sometimes have failed as a parent. But by practicing faith working through love you will help your child and yourself become more conformed to God's character, and God wants that even more than he wants flawless parenting. Also, as you and your children learn to value each other as Christ does, parenting will become more of the joy God intends.

Will you join us as we pray? Lord, give us eyes of faith to see our children as you see them—as precious jewels. Build in us a love that values everyone we meet, starting with our family and flowing outward like rivers of living water. Mold us into new creations who reveal your character to those around us. Set us free from habit patterns that devalue our children and ourselves and teach us how to have faith and trust in you. Make us vessels you can work through to bless our families and to help our children become godly men and women. You said, "If any of you lacks wisdom, let him ask God" (James 1:5). We ask for wisdom, Jesus. Pour your wisdom into our minds and hearts. We need you, Lord. Most importantly, help us know and love you more deeply than we ever thought possible. Thank you for loving and guiding us. We trust in your Word that says, "Thou wilt show me the path of life: in thy presence is fulness of joy" (Ps. 16:11 KJV). Help us to stay in your presence always, Lord. Amen.

Appendix A

Building Godly Character Game

When children have problems, parents often focus on the negative. Constantly focusing upon the faults of our children (and spouse) can cause pain and can destroy self-esteem. In addition, being critical often damages our relationships with those we criticize. How do we stop?

It does little good to concentrate all of our efforts on *not* doing something we want to stop. The most effective way to change is to concentrate on doing good in place of the bad.

This principle works well with building godly character in your children. Get the whole family involved. Make a chart with each person's name on it. Each person identifies a positive quality he or she wants to work on. If one says something negative like "not arguing," try to think of the positive opposite to strive for, such as speaking one's views respectfully. Smaller children may need some suggestions to choose from, such as speaking in a pleasant voice (opposite of whining), being generous, doing chores pleasantly, sharing, eating healthily, exercising, organizing and putting away items in their proper places, or any fruit of the Spirit (Gal. 5:22).

After the chart is made, have everyone in the family try to "catch" each other doing the good things. If you catch someone hanging up his or her clothes, say, "I'm giving you a star for organization!" and put a star on the chart by his or her name. Give stars even if the person does something good in an area he or she is not working on. At the end of the week, or after a certain number of stars, have a family game-night or do something fun together to celebrate. Then choose a new godly quality, or the same one, for the next week. Practice each new good behavior until it becomes a habit.

Name	Quality	Week 1	Week 2
Daddy	Family Time	*********	
Mama	Joy & Humor	********	
Child 1	Patience	*****	
Child 2	Cheerful Helping	**********	
Child 3	Sharing	****	

Appendix B

Come Running to Mama Game

It is important for children to come the first time parents call. This not only honors parents, but can be lifesaving if children are in danger. Train through praise, encouragement, games, stories, and example, whenever possible. This reduces the need for punishment and makes punishment more effective when it is used.

Use enthusiasm and make games fun. Say, "Let's play the 'Come-Running' game! I'll call you. Come the first time I call. Ready? Tracy, come here." Then clap your hands and hug Tracy as soon as she comes. Tell her that you'll play the "Come-Running" game several times during the day. Warn her, each time you get ready to call, "I'm going to call you now. Remember to come right away. Come here please." Each time Tracy comes, clap, hug, cheer. After the behavior is well learned, continue to play periodically as long as it is fun for her.

Once children understand that they need to come right away when called, *then* explain that if they do not come immediately when you call them, you must spank them (or whatever form of punishment you feel is best for this misbehavior). Administer any necessary punishment in love *before* you get angry, and be consistent. (See Table 4–2.) For a while, continue to warn, "I'm going to call you now." Have children tell you what will happen if they disobey. Then if they refuse to come, administer punishment.

When coming immediately is an ingrained habit, the warnings will no longer be necessary. However, periodically tell them you appreciate how they come when you call. Tell them how grown up they are and thank them for their obedience. Never take good behavior for granted, or it will disappear.

Appendix C

Follow Directions Game

Children need to follow directions not only for safety, but also for school and for jobs. This game teaches children to listen, make eye contact, and stretch their memory.

If a child is two or three, start with one or two directions. After you see that the child can remember what you say and do it, add an additional command, then more. Keep it simple to insure success.

Begin by saying, "Let's play the Follow Directions Game. I'll tell you something to do. Then you do what I say. Ready? Look at me. Pat your head, then wiggle your nose." The sillier the commands, the more fun it is. Demonstrate each action as you say it. If the child has trouble remembering the next command, help. Say, "Let's see. Was it wiggle your nose? Great job!" Praise, cheer, and encourage.

Older children can follow an entire obstacle course of directions, after they've been trained to listen. Let them give commands to you. Pretend to forget one of the directions (it might not be pretend) and then show them how to good-naturedly admit a mistake. If you model not getting upset by mistakes and trying again, they will learn to not fear failure and not be afraid to risk something new.

Vary this game by racing to pick up a certain color, shape, word, letter, etc. Children who have been trained to listen and follow instructions will succeed more at school and life.

Appendix D

Practice Game

This game is similar to the "Come Running to Mama" game. The purpose is to have fun while training young children in healthy habits. This reduces the need for punishment, thus making punishment more effective when it is needed.

If a child misbehaves, try this game. For example, assume your child draws on the walls. Take out paper and crayons and place them wherever you want the child to draw. Explain that he or she can draw on paper and not on walls. If crayons are accessible, but paper is not, the child will find a place to draw (often the wrong place), so have paper within easy reach for the child.

Next, take the child to the room where he or she just drew on the wall. Say, "Do we draw on the walls?" Shout together, "NO!" Ask, "Where do we draw?" Together, "We run for the paper!" Hold hands with your child and run (or walk fast) to the correct location, get out paper, and draw for a minute. Cheer. Hug. Praise.

Then take the child into another room. Repeat several times. When the child doesn't want to practice any more, say, "We need to practice so you draw on paper and not on walls. Do you know where to draw next time, or do we need to practice more?" If the child says he or she understands, ask, "Where will you draw next time?" "Paper." "Good!"

After practice, *every time* the child draws on paper, clap, cheer and specifically praise, "You remembered to draw on paper at the table! Great job!" Continue to give lots of attention for the correct behavior until the behavior is well established. Then periodic praise will be enough.

Use this game to practice any behavior that the child has trouble remembering. Practice helps build good habits, and so does praise.

Appendix E

Shopping Rules

Create three simple rules for stores. Each child must say every rule *before* going into the store, each time you go.

Rule 1: Do not touch. Little hands can damage merchandise and get hurt. Don't allow the child to touch an item on the shelf. After you have chosen an item, if it is safe, let a child hold something you plan to purchase. Bring toys, snacks, or a little baby buggy or shopping cart the child can push (loaded with some safe items). While children are riding in your cart, tie toys to your cart with a shoe lace for easy retrieval.

Rule 2: Do not ask for anything. "You may tell me your needs and desires before we get to the store. In the store, I will let you help me make some decisions. But if you ask for something in the store, the answer will be 'no,' even if it was something I had planned to buy." The reason for this rule is that store managers are smart. They put toys, candy, and sugar cereals at children's eye level. An adult cannot think of his or her list and do math to figure best buys if little voices constantly ask, "Can I have . . . ?" Parents also feel like ogres if they say "no" too often, so they often buy unhealthy items that their budget can't afford. If your rule says "No asking" then you can decide when to let children choose. "Would you like these apples or these oranges?" Give specific choices between acceptable alternatives.

Rule 3: Stay where I can see you and you can see me. Once children are old enough to get out of the grocery cart or stroller and can follow the "no touch" rule, they need to understand the importance of staying close to the parent to avoid kidnapping or harm to the child or to the store. If they break any rule, they immediately lose the privilege of walking and must get back in the cart, even if it means pushing two carts.

Give older children positive things to do, so they aren't tempted to misbehave. For example, play "I Spy." Say, "I spy something red. Can you guess what it is?" Let them find items pictured on coupons that you want to buy. Or ask, "Can you find artichokes (or any unusual item)?" Use shopping time to lovingly interact and teach.

References

Ainsworth, Mary D. S., M. Blehar, E. Waters, and S. Walls. 1978. *Patterns of attachment*. Hillsdale, N.J.: Erlbaum.

American Psychiatric Association. 1994. *Diagnostic and statistical manual of mental disorders*, 4th ed. Washington, D.C.: Author.

Anolik, S. A. 1983. Family influence upon delinquency: Biosocial and psychosocial perspectives. *Adolescence* 18:489–98.

Bates, J. E., and K. Bayles. 1988. Attachment and the development of behavior problems. In *Clinical implications of attachment*, ed. J. Belsky and T. Nexworski, pp. 253–94. Hillsdale, N.J.: Erlbaum.

Baumrind, D. 1967. Child care practices anteceding three patterns of preschool behavior. *Genetic Psychology Monographs* 75:43–88.

———. 1971. Current patterns of parental authority. *Developmental Psychology Monograph* 4 (No. 1, Pt. 2).

Belsky, J. 1988. The "effects" of infant day care reconsidered. *Early Childhood Research Quarterly* 3:235–72.

Belsky, J., and M. Rovine. 1985. Nonmaternal care in the first year of life and the security of the infant-parent attachment. *Child Development* 56:157–67.

Berger, K. S. 1988. *The developing person through the life span*, 2nd ed. New York: Worth Publishers, Inc.

Berk, L. E. 1993. *Infants, children, and adolescents*. Boston: Allyn and Bacon.

Bowlby, J. 1969. *Attachment*. New York: Basic Books.

Bradley, R. H., B. M. Caldwell, and S. L. Rock. 1988. Home environment and school performance: A ten-year follow-up and examination of three models of environmental action. *Child Development* 59:852–67.

Chalmers, J. B., and M. A. R. Townsend. 1990. The effects of training in social perspective taking on socially maladjusted girls. *Child Development* 61:179–90.

Christenson, L. 1970. *The Christian family*. Minneapolis, MN: Bethany Fellowship, Inc.

Collins, W. A., H. Wellman, A. H. Keniston, and S. D. Westby. 1978. Age-related aspects of comprehension and inference from a televised dramatic narrative. *Child Development* 49:389–99.

Emery, R. E. 1989. Family violence. *American Psychologist* 44:321–28.

Eyre, L., and R. Eyre. 1993. *Teaching your children values*. New York: Simon and Schuster.

Feshbach, N. D., and S. Feshbach. 1982. Empathy training and the regulation of aggression: Potentialities and limitations. *Academic Psychology Bulletin* 4:399–413.

Hetherington, E. M., and K. A. Camara. 1984. Families in transition: The process of dissolution and reconstitution. In *Review of child development research*, ed. Ross D. Parke, vol. 7. Chicago: University of Chicago Press.

Holden, G. W., and K. L. Ritchie. 1991. Linking extreme marital discord, child rearing, and child behavior problems: Evidence from battered women. *Child Development* 62:311–27.

Johnson, W. B. 1993. Father uninvolvement: Impact, etiology and potential solutions. *Journal of Psychology and Christianity* 12:301–11.

Liebert, R. M., and J. Sprafkin. 1988. *The early window: Effects of television on children and youth*, 3rd ed. New York: Paramon Press.

Montemayor, R. 1983. Parents and adolescents in conflict: All families some of the time and some families all of the time. *Journal of Early Adolescence* 3:83–103.

Rice, M. E., and J. E. Grusec. 1975. Saying and doing: Effects on observer performance. *Journal of Personality and Social Psychology* 32:584–93.

Rushton, J. P. 1975. Generosity in children: Immediate and long-term effects of modeling, preaching, and moral judgment. *Journal of Personality and Social Psychology* 31:459–66.